Grinding, Honing and Polishing

Grinding, Honing and Polishing

Stan Bray

Special Interest Model Books

Special Interest Model Books Ltd
P.O.Box 327
Poole, Dorset BH15 2RG
England

First published 2009
Reprinted 2010, 2017, 2019, 2021

© 2009 Stan Bray

ISBN 978 185486 252 5

www.specialinterestmodelbooks.co.uk

Printed and bound by Melita Press, Malta

Contents

Introduction

We are all familiar with grinding in some form or another and to anyone involved in mechanical engineering it is a subject that is essential. The process could in its simplest form be described as rubbing one surface against another in order to wear one, or in some cases both, down. The wear may be in order to reduce an object to a required size, to shape, to produce a smooth or polished finish or, as is more often the case for an engineer, to sharpen a tool. The amount of friction and therefore wear involved will depend on the materials used to actually do the grinding and the material that is being ground. It will also depend on the reason that material is being ground.

It is not known when the human race first discovered the use of the grinding process but it has certainly been in use for many thousands of years. Stone Age man is known to have polished items for use as jewellery and the sharpening of weapons has seemingly been going on almost since the human race first evolved.

Sharpening of tools and weapons has always been a major use for grinding and this means that the material used for grinding must be harder than the material being sharpened. If the grinding medium is too soft it will take a very long time indeed to sharpen the tool and a great deal of the abrasive material will itself be worn away. All the materials regularly used for grinding are indeed very hard but that in itself is not the final answer. How rough they are will also be a major factor. The rougher the abrasive material used for sharpening, the quicker the process will be, but also because of its coarseness the finished result will be in itself rough. Such a finish might well be suitable for a cold chisel or an axe, whether the latter is used for felling trees or in battle, but is not likely to be suitable for a fine edged sword or a surgeon's knife. Using a smoother material will mean a longer time is taken to sharpen the object but the finished result will be a much finer finish and therefore a keener edge. The obvious solution is to use a coarse grinding material first, followed by a finer one and in many instances a progression of grinding material is used to obtain the required finish.

If we take this a little further and use an ultra fine medium for the grinding process, the sharpening process will take a disproportional amount of time, but by using such a medium the material can be highly polished. For example, to polish an object such as a brass button, a polishing material is applied. That material might well contain a solvent of some sort to remove tarnish but it will also contain a mild abrasive. It was not unusual in the days when soldiers were required to wear uniforms with brightly polished buttons for the motif on the button to be gradually worn completely away as a result of the polishing. This demonstrates that grinding and polishing are in fact identical processes, differing only by the medium used and possibly the amount of time involved in completing the process.

We are not concerned here with sharpening weapons, or with polishing buttons either, but we are interested in sharpening tools and applying a polished finish to various objects, processes that in many ways are similar. In addition to sharpening simple tools and polishing metal this book is concerned with precision grinding by machine, the precisian grinding machine having become an indispensable machine in most engineering workshops, no matter what their class of work. It makes very little difference whether it be work demanding the closest accuracy or fine finish. By the use of grinding machines instead of older types of machine, processes can often be simplified and greater accuracy obtained. That said it should be pointed out that grinding machines are not necessarily the best for repetition work. Most are very simple to operate and in many cases require less setting up than other machines. This means less time switching from one job to another. As well as grinding and polishing we will also go into lapping and honing, two very similar processes, both of which rely on a form of grinding.

The replacement of a steel tool by a grinding wheel was first adapted to deal with the problem of hardened work and when it was necessary to correct pieces that had been distorted by heat. The advantages of using a machine to grind work instead of one to turn or mill it was soon realized and has resulted in big improvement in engineering standards. For example, on an ordinary motor car there are now numerous parts that are ground to size and shape, with the result that modern cars need far less maintenance and run much smoother than vehicles built fifty or more years ago.

At one time although grinding gave more accurate results than turning and produced a superior surface, the time taken by the process did not make it worth while and was generally confined to work needing a very high degree of accuracy and finish. With the introduction of better quality grinding wheels and improved machines the process became transformed and it is now used in instances where at one time turning and milling would have been the order of the day.

This applies particularly to cylindrical grinding where the lathe just cannot compete for accuracy or quality of finish with the cylindrical grinding machine. Duplication of work such as crankshaft journals is far easier on a grinding machine than it is with a lathe. The same can be said for the machining of flat material where the finish obtained by surface grinding will invariably be far better than could ever hope to be obtained when using a normal milling machine. Yet another advantage of grinding machines is the fact that on the whole they are easier to set up than the more usual machine tools.

We must not forget the various other operations involving the grinding process, albeit they generally call for far less accuracy than does the use of a grinding machine. Nevertheless, the use of mounted points, abrasive papers and all the various other operations that are dealt with within these pages are all most important and form a valuable part of general engineering practice. At one time grinding materials were invariably natural ones. Modern technology now means that most are artificial and generally far more efficient that the older materials. The range available is now vast and it is hoped to introduce the reader to most.

One strange anomaly when dealing with the subject of grinding material is that the name given to many tools is 'a sanding something or other,' when often the operation involved does not involve the use of sandpaper or cloth of any sort, which is mainly used by woodworkers. Readers should therefore take note that although the name of a tool might be preceded by the word sanding, that does not mean that it can only be used for woodworking.

Processes such as honing and lapping will also be dealt with. These are fine grinding processes used as a means of getting as near a perfect fit to two mating parts as possible, the most common example being the fitting of a piston in a cylinder. If a cylinder is not bored accurately and with a good smooth finish to the bore it will be ineffective and wasteful of fuel. Tiny ridges remain after normal boring operations are complete and these provide a means of the propulsion gas or liquid to escape along the sides of the piston. Honing takes out those ridges, providing a much smoother bore to the cylinder and so there is less chance of an escape.

Finally it should be noted that most of the photographs in the book show grinding operations apparently taking place without suitable safety guards being in position. The photographs were staged for the purpose of clarity and at all times any use of a grinding wheel requires an adequate guard to be in position.

Stan Bray 2009

Chapter One

Materials

As mentioned in the introduction, within reason almost any material can be used for grinding or polishing although the material must be harder than that which it is used on. For example, a knife can be honed to a fine edge on a piece of concrete or a paving stone. The same material could be used to impart a polish but when it comes to polishing a softer material is sometimes used. Cooking pots are often scoured with nylon scourers; the scourer is not just removing unwanted remains of the cooking process, but is actually imparting a polished finish to the utensil as well. We are all aware that the nylon will rapidly wear away but in doing so it is removing minute pieces of utensil in order to give it that polish. The nylon therefore can just as easily be used to impart a polished finish to a piece of metal, even though it is apparently softer than the piece being worked on. The principal of grinding, polishing, etc therefore is that the work is done by friction, the medium used is an essential aid to that process and by careful selection of material it is possible to carry out these operations with the maximum efficiency.

The best materials to use for various grinding and polishing operations have been established over the years and have

These small grindstones are called grinding points and are available in a wide variety of shapes, sizes and materials. The three shown here because they clearly demonstrate how various types of material can be recognised by their colour.

also been allied to other materials to improve their efficiency. These abrasive materials may be formed into grind stones by bonding them in various ways as well as stuck to paper or cloth or simply mixed with some form of liquid (usually but not always oil) in order to form a suitable grinding paste. Knowledge of the material means that the various grinding processes can be carried out with the maximum efficiency so let us have a look at some of them at least. There are hundreds of different types of abrasive and describing every type and what it is best used for is not possible, so only those likely to be used in the home workshop, some of which are common and some of which are not quite so common, will be dealt with.

With a few exceptions, such as the nylon scourer, all of the various substances used for grinding are crushed to form, or manufactured as small grains and each has its own peculiarities, some of the grains being harder than others. Having obtained grains of the required size, a lot of care is then taken to stick them all back together, one way or another. Details of how they are stuck together or bonded will be given in due course. In use the grains are designed to break away from the bonding material leaving new ones continually exposed. Because of this they are described as friable and the fact that they do break away means that new sharp ones are constantly replacing those that have become blunt. This effect is particularly useful when working on hard materials such as carbide and high-speed steel. In order to remove the grains that have been used, some form of lubricant is usually desirable when grinding. This not only cools the work and the stone but also washes away the spent particles, leaving sharp ones exposed.

Some of the materials are natural but mostly modern abrasives are of manufactured materials. Grindstones work on this principal of continually exposing small sharp particles of the material to the item being sharpened. Where grinding material is allied to paper and cloth, the process of replacement with sharp material is not always the case. Many inexpensive papers and cloths have only a single layer of material and once this is used the cloth or paper is discarded. Some of the better quality sheets may have a second or third layer but needless to say the life of any paper or cloth is inevitably limited.

Sandstone

Sandstone is well known as a building material and contains quartz as well as silica. The content of the latter can be quite high and the higher it is the better, as it will work as a grinding material. At one time sandstone was extensively used for making millstones etc. It was also used for grinding wheels used to sharpen farm implements as well as woodworking tools. Grindstones made of sandstone were to be seen in blacksmiths' forges and carpenters shops, they also found their way into engineering factories. Most of this type of grindstone were manufactured from solid sandstone rather than from grains; almost invariably the stones were of a large diameter, frequently rotated by hand in a bath of water.

Many were very roughly made - the shaft that went through the centre was often nothing more that a piece of wrought iron forged to shape running in holes cut in thick steel plates that formed the sides of the set up. This hardly resulted in an accurate machine. The plates would have a strip welded to them and this would form the bath into which water was poured. The fact that the stone was running in water washed away worn particles and kept new sharp pieces on the surface to do their job. However it was usual for the water to remain in the trough and the grindstone was therefore constantly wet on one edge. No doubt because of the bad form of construction, the stone would be out of balance and every time it was left out of use exactly the same part of the stone would remain soaking in water. Sandstone is a material formed by nature and as the name suggests it is merely sand that has been compressed. This continual immersion in water tended to undo nature's work and soak out some of the natural binding of the stone. The result would be that some sections were hard and others soft and uneven and so not capable of doing the job the stone was intended for. Nevertheless it was good enough for sharpening scythes and similar implements but was not under those conditions a great deal of good for sharpening machine tools.

These types of grindstone are usually now obsolete and more likely to be seen in a museum, although it may be possible some do remain on farms where they may be convenient in situations a long way from electrical supplies.

Glass

At one time paper and cloth layered with grains of fine glass were used, generally for woodwork (the material being less suitable for use on metal). Readers will not be surprised to learn this was known as glass paper; manufactured in this way it is now extremely rare. The name however persists and we do find papers sold for woodworking as glass paper even though the abrasive material is not necessarily glass.

Flint

A type of quartz found in rocks, flint was used as an abrasive material as long ago as the Stone Age. In more recent times it has been used in conjunction with flexible materials to make sandpaper. Although still popular for use in woodworking it has little real place in metalworking.

Emery

An impure form of corundum with a high degree of hardness, emery is possibly the best known of all abrasive materials. There is one problem and that is the fact it is not consistent in its hardness and two apparently identical examples are likely to behave in a completely differently manner.

Corundum

A popular abrasive for coating papers and cloth and also for making into wheels, this material is naturally occurring and is closely allied to hard jewel stones of various types.

Garnet

Another naturally occurring material that is widely used for coating paper and making disks, garnet is also quite commonly used in powder form mixed with some form of lubricant as a grinding paste, as well as for honing and polishing.

Aluminium oxide

Made from bauxite, aluminium oxide consists of blunt shaped grains and is very tough in its lowest refined form. During the melting stage in the production of aluminium oxide, the crystalline structure and its chemistry can be controlled, allowing the manufacturer to produce a family of products that perform differently. Aluminium oxide is produced in a variety of types, and its versatility makes it the most commonly used abrasive. Many forms also contain a small quantity of titanium making it particularly effective when used with very hard materials.

White fused aluminium oxide

White Fused Aluminium Oxide is softer, or more friable, than ordinary aluminium oxide or many other abrasives. It has high chemical purity that gives it a cool, fast-cutting action; a particular asset is the fact that it holds its form well. It is particularly useful for grinding heat-sensitive metals. This is because of the fact that it generates less heat than other grinding materials it is often favoured for grinding heat-treated tool steels and high speed steels. It is also useful when grinding internally such as in cylinders because of the fact that less heat is generated.

Aluminium oxide with chrome oxide

A material with a distinctive pink colour that is a little tougher than white fused aluminium oxide. Like fused white aluminium oxide, it is comparatively cool when used but has the additional advantage of holding its shape well. For this reason it is frequently used in tool rooms for grinding hard alloy steels.

High chromium aluminium oxide

High chromium aluminium oxide is a dark reddish coloured abrasive that is made by fusing high purity calcined alumina and chromium oxide. It is tougher than the more common white aluminium oxide. Wheels made from this tend to hold their shape well and in particular there is less rounding off of the corners of such wheels. It is used a great deal by engineering companies specialising in high quality grinding operations and is useful for both surface and cylindrical grinding.

Silicon carbide

A synthetic material produced from quartz and powdered petroleum coke, which is crushed to form the abrasive material. It is very hard and brittle with the result that when made into wheels and disks there is a constant replenishing of sharp material as the original is worn away. It is particularly useful on materials with a low tensile strength.

Black silicon carbide

A semi friable medium-density abrasive, black silicon carbide is used for both resin and vitrified wheels and points. Its main use is for grinding hard or brittle materials such as cast iron, ceramics and glass. However, its use is not necessarily confined to working on such materials as it also is used for grinding brass and copper.

Green silicon carbide

This is the highest purity silicon carbide and is a medium density, friable abrasive that is mainly used in vitrified, bonded points and wheels. Until the advent of diamond bonded abrasives it was the only form that was recommended for sharpening cemented carbide tools. It is an abrasive that remains comparatively cool in use, which is another reason why it was used for this purpose.

Diamonds.

Both natural and synthetic diamonds are used as abrasives, in the form of wheels and disks. They are crushed into fine pastes for polishing and in that form are often used by clockmakers. Diamonds are used to make both vitrified and resin bonded wheels, the former are more fragile than the resin bonded type but cut more freely. Diamonds are often bonded to metal disks for use on cut-off wheels as well as for cup wheels and other situations where high mechanical strength is required.

Cubic boron nitride

Generally referred to as CBN, this material is nearly as hard as the diamond and has a greater thermal stability that makes it suitable for use where cooling can be a problem. It is commonly used in the production of diesel and petrol engines where it is used for crankshaft grinding, these frequently being made from chilled cast iron. In fact the material finds favour in industry where it is necessary to grind materials that are unsuitable for grinding

with the more normal materials. CBN is produced in a number of grades and a special glass bonding has been developed to improve the strength of wheels made with the material.

Fibres

All the above are materials that we generally accept as those used for grinding and polishing purposes. There is however a large group that we must not ignore and this consists of fibrous materials of various sorts. We are all familiar with such material when used for household scouring pads and of course such a pad is capable of imparting a polish to a metal object. Much more durable material of a similar sort is available that has been designed especially for use in engineering. It is available as pads or sheets and also as wheels of different types. The actual material used to manufacture these items varies, but these days most are man made fibres. Many are very durable and are not only capable of polishing but can also be used to remove small amounts of metal, if necessary.

So there are a number of different materials likely to be found in use for grinding of various types, some industries use other material where the situation demands.

Chapter Two

Grinding Wheels

Although all sorts of grinding processes come within the remit of this book, in particular we must deal with grinding wheels: how to know what each will do, how to look after them and of course how to use them.

Wheel speeds
The maximum operating rotational peripheral speed" of a grinding wheel depends on the type of bond and the size and type of grain. The maximum speed will always be marked on the wheel by the manufacturer and should under no circumstances be exceeded. To exceed the speed is very dangerous and can result in not only damage to the wheel but also serious injury to the operator.

Construction of wheels
A knowledge of how wheels are made and the materials used will be a help in understanding why we need to do certain things when they are used, so the following few paragraphs will deal with the construction methods

It gives one a nice safe feeling to know

The maximum speed at which a grindstone should be used is printed on a label fitted to the side of the stone. Under no circumstances should this speed be exceeded.

for the proposed wheels. In actual fact the rings are slightly larger to allow for the dressing of the wheels. The rings are placed in a drying room and when considered dry enough to handle the bonded material is removed from the forming ring. A machine similar to a potter's wheel is used next, to get the wheels to the required shape after which they are placed in a drying room until thoroughly dry. From there they are put in a kiln and baked at a temperature of approximately sixteen hundred degrees Celcius. This process takes a couple of weeks, depending on the size and number of wheels, which in turn to some extent also dictates the size of kiln. After removal they are tried and tested for soundness; this test also depends on the grading of the wheel. Wheels made in this way are particularly useful for general workshop practice as they have a high resistance to oil water and acids. They are also less prone to problems than those with a silicate bond when the temperature of them is raised. In addition they have a certain amount of elasticity, which adds to their life.

that if we follow the details on the label and mount grinding wheels properly nothing should go wrong and we probably need do no more than go to the local tool stockist and order a fine, medium or coarse wheel. Up to a point that will be true. A good stockist will be able to supply a wheel suitable for general grinding purposes, but he or she should be able to do a great deal more than that. Not only are there many different types of grit that can be used for specific purposes, but just as important is the material used to bond those grits together in order to form them into wheels and the following will give readers some idea of the type of bond that might be required for a specific purpose.

Vitrified bond

This type of bond is the most commonly used and it is generally used for tool grinding. In the case of a vitrified bond, the abrasive material and the materials used to form the bond are mixed with water to form a plastic mass. When it is all thoroughly mixed it is put into iron rings of approximately the size required

Elastic bond

So-called elastic bond is a name used to describe several synthetic processes used for bonding, all of which are similar to the above (the difference being in the material that is used). The finished result is a wheel that as the name suggests is more flexible or elastic. It is a particularly

18

useful type of bond when wheels are to be used for polishing rather than grinding, typical examples being Scotbright and Brightboy, wheels that are designed for this purpose. The colour of a wheel with an elastic bond will depend on its type and such wheels are usually recognisable by the fact that they can be bent slightly by hand. Elastic bonds certainly have many uses but they also have one big disadvantage that is the fact that they have a limited life span. After a period of time the bond becomes liable to break down and using a wheel in this condition could be dangerous. Some manufacturers put a date on the label, after which it is deemed unwise to use the wheel.

Rubber bond

The most common type of elastic bond and, as the name suggests, given to wheels bonded with rubber, which can be either natural or synthetic. During manufacture the rubber is vulcanised to whatever degree of hardness is required for that particular type of wheel. This bond is suitable for cut off wheels and wheels used for special purposes. It is a bond that is frequently used to make the miniature wheels used for die grinding. Here again we have a bond that is liable to break down after a period of time and care needs to be taken to ensure this time is not exceeded.

Shellac bond

Another elastic type, this is a bond of ordinary natural shellac. The wheels have a good elasticity while not being truly flexible and are mainly used on work requiring a particularly high degree of finish. They are also used for slitting and

slotting purposes. Shellac bonding is also generally used to make wheels that consist of natural or synthetic diamond grains.

Although the elastic type of bonds are not ideal for normal work such as that done with an off hand grinder, they have great strength and as the name implies considerable elasticity. They are frequently found as specially shaped wheels and can be made as thin as 1.5mm and so find a place in workshops for special purposes for which the more usually bonded wheels are less suitable.

Silicate bond

In this case the abrasive material is mixed with clay and silicate of soda and when the mix reaches a plastic state it is put in moulds that are then baked at a much lower temperature than that used for the vitrified bond. The length of time that they are baked for is also much less, being typically around twenty-four hours. The treatment after removal from the kiln is the same as that used when making wheels with a vitrified bond. This type of wheel is generally used where it is not possible to have a good supply of coolant. Even so, the wheel must not be used in such a way that too much heat is generated as doing so can cause it to disintegrate.

Resinoid bond

The name resinoid bond refers to wheels made with a synthetic resin and they are particularly suitable for use at very high speeds. They can be run at over nine thousand revolutions per minute with safety. Because of this capability, this type of wheel is commonly used for cut off wheels.

The reverse side of this wheel has a label giving all the information required to assist one in selecting the right wheel. This type of label is not found on all wheels; some only have the main label giving speeds, grit, etc.

Selecting the right wheel

It has already been described how all grinding materials work on the principal of constant exposure of the grit. This applies to grinding wheels and the grade of the wheel indicates its ability to retain or release the abrasive grains. This in turn is usually associated with the type, size and density of the grains as well as the type of bond that has been used to manufacture the wheel. The ideal wheel grade is one that increases the release of the abrasives as the grinding forces increase, an example of this being the sharpening of a tool with a particularly blunt edge. If a wheel is too soft, excessive wheel wear occurs while a wheel that is too hard will result in a dulling effect of the grains causing the wheel to glaze over rather than continually expose new cutting edges. This will result in a lower cutting ability and unnecessary heating of the work piece.

The structure of the wheel is indicated on the label by a symbol and denotes the density of the grains, i.e. the spaces between them. It must be remembered that the grains standing proud of the bonding material have air between and it is these spaces that to a large extent govern the operation of the wheel. This structure is controlled during the manufacturing process and the purpose of varying structures is to provide suitable spacing between the grains that will reduce or prevent clogging of the wheel. The spacings have been carefully calculated to suit various materials and it is desirable that the correct wheel is used that will suit the material being ground. The size of the individual grains decides the rate of metal removal. Large grains will remove more material than smaller ones, and wheels used for this purpose also need the grains at wider spacings than those designed for a lesser removal rate.

A word of warning here, as it is possible to purchase cheap grinding wheels that do not have a suitable label affixed. They are often sold on market stalls and shops specialising in cheap goods. The use of these wheels is inadvisable; they can be dangerous and will only give inferior results.

Mounting wheels

It is essential that the shafts on which wheels are mounted run true and are fitted in good bearings and although in the case of cheaper machines plain bearings might

20

This photograph shows the correct way to mount a grindstone, note the paper washer can just be seen behind the cup washer, the nut must not be over tightened, at the same time it must be tight enough for the wheel to be secure. It is essential that wheels be always properly mounted.

be used, ideally the shaft should run on ball or needle roller bearings. Most modern wheels are designed to run at very high speeds, which in turn demands, the use of good quality bearings. We will come to the various types of machines where wheels are used but no matter what the machine is, the wheel must be correctly mounted. Many will come with a central mounting hole that will be too large for the spindle on which it is to be fitted. With the wheel should come an insert or perhaps inserts made of plastic. These are fitted in the central hole of the stone, the hole in the insert being the correct size for the shaft. Supplying them in this form means the manufacturer can make a single type of wheel of a given diameter that will fit most machines.

Because wheels are fragile and fracture easily, a cup washer of suitable diameter must be used on each side of the wheel to support it over a large area of the diameter. We have seen how the wheels are made by binding together grit particles and this in itself makes them quite fragile, although they may not look it. A wheel breaking up at high speed is a very dangerous prospect indeed. The washers used for the purpose ensure that the pressure on the stone is even. A plain washer might well result in greater pressure being applied in one place than in another.

A washer of paper or thin card must be placed between the cup washer and the wheel. This not only is an aid in ensuring even pressure all round, but is also ensures that the hard surface of the cup washer does not dig into the surface

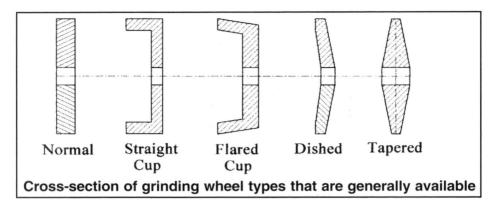

| Normal | Straight Cup | Flared Cup | Dished | Tapered |

Cross-section of grinding wheel types that are generally available

of the wheel. Most wheels that are likely to be used by the model engineer will be straight sided, however some types of work call for the sides to be tapered. A tapered wheel demands a special tapered washer to ensure the even sideways pressure is maintained on the wheel. Generally the manufacturer of the wheel can supply suitable washers. Under no circumstances should a wheel be used without the side support of the washers.

Special tool grinding wheels

For the purpose of grinding tools such as milling cutters, etc, wheels are made in a cup shape. This allows the grinding process to be carried out on the edge of the wheel where there is the greatest strength. The cups can take a variety of shapes, some are quite shallow, others deep; in addition to providing a flat grinding surface these also have the advantage that better vision of the tool set up is available. Some, in particular those with a deep recess can be quite fragile and extra care is needed when mounting them as they are prone to breakage. The metal cup

A cup wheel, usually used on a tool and cutter grinder. This type of wheel allows the periphery to be used for sharpening. At the same time there is no unwanted radius so the tool edges can be ground flat.

washer and cardboard washers should be large enough to support the whole of the central area of the cup, which is flat. The wheels chip easily on the periphery and under no circumstances should a wheel that has chipped be used until the chip has been dressed out.

Diamond coated wheels

The modern trend for tool and cutter grinding is to use diamond-coated wheels. They are cup shaped in a similar way to ordinary cup wheels, but whereas the whole of a bonded wheel consists of the

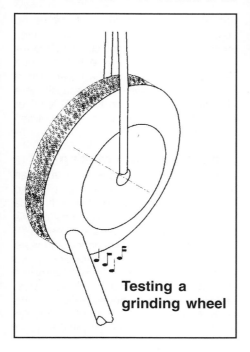

Testing a grinding wheel

same material, diamond wheels have the grinding surface only on the edges that will be used to do the work. The stones, which sometimes are synthetic material rather than diamonds, are bonded to a former of pressed fibre or similar material. There are obvious advantages in their use as far as the grinding operation is concerned; in addition the whole wheel is considerably stronger than the normal bonded type.

Testing grinding wheels

Because wheels are fragile and break easily they must be treated with care and should not be allowed to fall. Before use, they should be carefully examined for cracks or other signs of damage and if

A very coarse grain wheel that is beginning to show signs of breaking up. In all probability as well as having been misused it has a bond with a limited life. It is certainly time for it to be discarded.

damage of any sort is discovered they must be discarded. A good general test for soundness is to support the wheel on a loop of string and gently tap it with a pierce of metal, if a ringing sound ensues, the wheel will be sound, if the sound emitted is dull then it must be treated with suspicion as almost certainly it will be cracked and in danger of breaking up in use. Most wheels should be stored in a dry place on edge, thin straight-sided wheels as well as those shellac and rubber-bonded however should be laid down on a flat surface to prevent warping.

Break up of grinding wheels

Almost certainly the greatest danger when grinding is the possibility of a wheel breaking up during operations. It is quite a frightening prospect as the effect is for the wheel to literally explode. It fragments into numerous pieces of varying size and the centrifugal force of the rotation is such that the pieces are capable of travelling considerable distances. If we bear in mind the fact that a wheel consists of thousands of tiny sharp particles of extremely hard material, it does not take a great deal of imagination to realise what one or more of those pieces can do to bare flesh, or even flesh covered with some flimsy material such as a shirt.

The reasons for breaking up

Any object that is made to rotate has additional stresses applied to it in two areas, radially and across the width, it is the former that mainly concerns us. As speed increases, so do the stresses. If we take a hypothetical situation and were to spin a steel disk at a fast enough speed it would eventually burst from the stresses imposed upon it. To make matters worse, as far as grinding wheels are concerned greater stresses are set up in a disc with a hole in the centre than one without. If that

is not sufficient, pressing a shaft into the hole increases the stress level even more. It now starts to become clear why grinding wheels are given a maximum speed rating and it must not be exceeded.

The formula used for working out such stresses is known as Poisson's Ratio but as far as general workshop practice is concerned it is best to follow the speed restrictions printed on the wheel by the manufacture.

How to dress grinding wheels

The nature of grindstones ensures that they are likely to become less effective. Blunting of the grains soon causes the wheel to become glazed, a condition in which it will not do its job properly. Constant sharpening of some tools can cause grooves to appear and general misuse may even cause edges to become ragged and chipped. To correct and prevent these problems the wheel should be dressed and we do this with a diamond-dressing tool.

The tools come in a number of types, the cheapest being what amounts to a

quantity of small diamond pieces stuck together to form a block. While not exactly high tech, these are quite effective and for the person who will rarely use a grindstone could be the perfect answer. A single point diamond tool is what the name says, a piece of steel rod with a diamond set in the end and multipoint tools simply have a number of diamonds usually mounted in the form of a plate. Diamond dressing tools should always be used at an angle to the wheel face. In fact they should be used at two angles. The first is an angle on a vertical plane, known generally as

The photograph shows a single point diamond dressing tool. It should always be used at an angle as detailed in the text. If it is used flat, the diamond will lose its edge and tend to make grooves in the wheel instead of dressing it across the face.

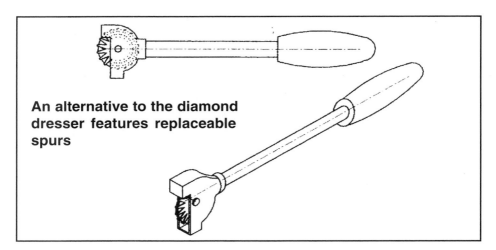

An alternative to the diamond dresser features replaceable spurs

canting; the second is an angle to the horizontal.

Canting is done in order to prevent the tool from chattering, which makes it impossible to obtain an even finish to the wheel. The point of the tool should be at the exact centre height of the wheel and the cant angle around five to ten degrees. The horizontal angle needs to be steeper and should be somewhere between twenty and thirty degrees and is used to prevent the tool digging in to the face of the wheel. An additional bonus is that using it at such an angle ensures that a point remains on the tool. If it is held exactly in line with the wheel face, the point of the tool will quickly wear away. When dressing a wheel it is essential to ensure that the

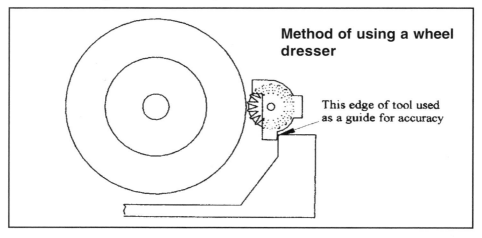

Method of using a wheel dresser

This edge of tool used as a guide for accuracy

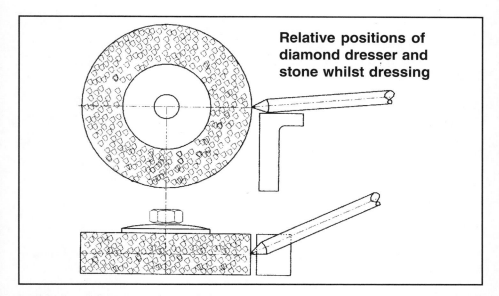

Relative positions of diamond dresser and stone whilst dressing

grains are completely fractured, otherwise it will not do its job. All debris should be completely cleaned up after a wheel has been dressed as the dust that remains is highly abrasive and therefore if left lying around will cause damage to bearings of other machines.

Grinding points

Grinding points are small self-contained grindstones made of various types of grit and in numerous shapes. Similar items have been used for many years to make high quality machine dies and similar tools. They are complete with their own mandrel and can be very convenient in certain situations. Apart from the very cheap ones, most are bonded in such a way that they can be rotated at a much higher speed than the normal grindstone. They are particularly useful for use in a powered hand drill and the variety of shapes available means that they can be used in situations where it may be impossible to use other tools.

Chapter Three

Surface Coated Abrasives

The term surface coated abrasives is generally applied to materials where the abrasive grains have been stuck to the surface of a flexible material that provides the backing. The adhesives most commonly used for this purpose are resin-based glues or those made from animal hide. Under this title come items such as abrasive paper, cloths, etc where the flexible material is covered with a single layer of abrasive. Most commonly known of these are sand paper and emery papers. In fact they are so common that many other types of flexible abrasives are commonly referred to by these names, rather as at one time all vacuum cleaners were known as Hoovers, irrespective of the company that actually made them. There have been many advances in the manufacture of these materials and there is now a very wide range of products, many of which are designed for use on particular types of metal. While the backing material may well still be paper or cloth, the use of a compressed fibre base material is also quite common, particularly where the end product is likely to see heavy or extensive use.

In many cases where there is to be heavy usage the grains are adhered to the back via an electrolytic process, which is more robust than the more normal method of bonding with adhesive. Having some knowledge of these modern materials (which are closely related to their early ancestors) enables one to use the material most suited to a particular purpose. Abrasive sheets are mainly used either to polish or obtain a fine finish on work, but also have their uses for removing small amounts of metal to allow a suitable fit to be made. When used on a soft material such as brass it is necessary to be careful to avoid scratching, which can

Abrasive cloth is available in strips like these two that are of different grades. Strips come in a variety of widths from very narrow to very wide. They are also available in lengths that vary from about six inches to whole rolls several metres in length.

be the result of uneven wear of the abrasive grains. Sometimes rubbing chalk over the surface of the abrasive medium before using it can prevent this. Once a soft metal has been scored removing the score marks can be very difficult.

Uses of materials

The development of different types of grains means that the maximum benefit can be obtained from each. For use on wood, sandpaper, which in many instances is made with flint grains, will give the best results. Garnet paper also works well on this medium. Aluminium oxide has now generally replaced the old fashioned emery, although that is still available. Quite frequently other abrasives are added to aluminium oxide, in which case it may well be sold under a trade name. It also appears in a variety of colours. Aluminium oxide is particularly efficient for working on metal of all types, but some varieties with special additives are sold that are specifically designed for working on particular metals such as stainless steel.

The descriptions "abrasive paper" and "abrasive cloths" are of course self explanatory, one type having a paper backing the other cloth. Both have their uses. The papers with a suitable grit are widely used in woodworking processes as paper can easily be folded neatly round a block, giving a nice wide flat surface to do the work. Papers are also used in engineering, depending largely on the type of work being carried out. The use of cloth tends to be more common as the cloth backed sheets stand up better to the harsher environment of the metal workshop. It will all depend very much on the particular situation; for the polishing of small parts, paper can often be more suitable as it is easier to handle than cloth backed sheets which of necessity are thicker than paper. It is quite usual for the operator to cut the paper to a suitable size and shape for the job in hand and also it is frequently folded round a file in order to obtain a good flat finish. Woodworkers frequently will fold sandpaper round a cork block and use it in that fashion. The use of cork rather than wood for this purpose allows a little more flexibility. It is hardly surprising to learn that these blocks are called sanding blocks. On the other hand, while cloth is frequently also used with a file in that way, it is much more difficult to fold to a square edge as one can when using paper. A particular advantage of using cloth is when working on a component of an awkward shape. In those conditions paper will frequently tear, while

Most abrasive papers can be bought either as individual sheets or in packets such as this. The packets may contain a single or several grades of the material. In this case the paper is silicone carbide, designed to be used either wet or dry.

cloth will stand up to rougher handling. A common use for cloth is to tear it into strips in order to polish curved surfaces by pulling it to and from round the circumference of the curve. Pressed fibre-backed material behaves in a similar fashion to cloth but has to be cut to shape rather than torn. A distinct advantage of this is that it does not fray at the edges after cutting, where as cloth may well do so.

If a flat area is to be worked on, the best way to use either cloth or paper is to lay a complete sheet on a known flat surface, such as a surface plate, and rub the work on it using a figure of eight movement. The reason for the shape of the movement is to ensure that the surface being worked on remains in a flat plane throughout the operation. If the work is moved too and from almost certainly a rocking movement will be set up and the piece will have rounded edges. Using a circular motion rather than the figure of eight is a little more successful than the too and from action but even then there is every chance that slightly more pressure will be applied to the one side of the circle, again creating an uneven finish. It is best to use an abrasive with a cloth backing for this sort of work.

Although there is a wide range of material used for the coatings, most papers and cloths sold in sheet form are usually described as silicone carbide or sandpaper. For most general work this is quite

satisfactory as it is only the grade and spacing of the grains that will be important. The backing will vary and should be chosen to suit the work it is to be used for. Light work requires nothing more than a thin paper while heavy duty will require either a heavier paper or cloth, or even pressed carbon.

In addition to being available in the form of sheets, cloth-backed abrasives can also be obtained in strip form, the strips being of varying widths. They are usually sold either as a complete roll or as a length cut from a roll. The strips can prove to be very useful and save the chore of cutting larger sheets to size.

Waterproof sheets

Specially manufactured paper that is waterproof is available and is commonly referred to as Wet and Dry. This waterproof paper is very useful for many purposes and as the name suggests can be used

Abrasive cloth moulded round a sponge rubber centre. Although more likely to be used by a builder or decorator, these block do have their uses in an engineering workshop. They can be used wet or dry.

either wet or dry. For general workshop practice it is most likely to be used dry, in the same way as the normal silicone carbide material. It is also possible to use it soaked in oil and doing so gives a good finish on mild steel, but the idea is not recommended for cast iron or non-ferrous metals. It is also inadvisable to use it in this way on work that is later to be silver soldered, brazed or welded as the oil remains in the work and will prevent good adhesion. This type of material is very popular in the motor industry, particularly for bodywork repairs. Used wet on paintwork that needs to be smoother or removed, it is possible by using a fine grade when wet to obtain an absolute feather edge finish to the area that is being dealt with. Like all forms of abrasive sheets, wet and dry is available in a wide variety of grades and should be used progressively from coarse to the finest available grade.

Buffing sticks

The idea of folding paper round a file in order to provide stability and a good flat surface has already been mentioned and

in fact readily prepared pieces of wood that have paper stuck to them are available commercially and are called buffing sticks. They probably will find most use amongst watch and clock makers, where there is a need to obtain both a fine finish and probably also to remove small amounts of metal in order to obtain a perfect fit between mating parts. Even so it is not unknown for them to be used in industry for the same purpose and they certainly can have a place in the home workshop. Of course anyone can stick a piece of abrasive paper round a length of flat wood and achieve a reasonable result. Buffing sticks take things a stage further than this. The wood is specially prepared with sharp ninety-degree corners and the paper used is extra thin to ensure a perfect fit to the wood. In addition the adhesive is applied in such a way that the paper fits absolutely smoothly to the wood, giving an absolutely flat surface on all four edges. The sticks are available in various grades.

Other forms of coated abrasives

While paper and cloth may be the most familiar form in which we find surface coated abrasives, they are used for numerous other purposes. For example, the use of buffing sticks has been referred to but it is also possible to obtain the abrasive wrapped around a sponge. The abrasive in this case is designed to be

Described as a polishing block, these blocks are made from grains loosely bonded with a flexible bond material. They come in a range of grits and are particularly useful when working in inaccessible areas. It is also possible to cut pieces from them in order to make small shaped blocks for particular purposes.

used wet or dry and the sponge has the advantage of allowing it to be used on radii as well as on flat surfaces. In addition to their use for engineering purposes such blocks are popular amongst DIY enthusiasts for smoothing paintwork prior to repainting. They are available in various grades. As well as square blocks, this type of abrasive can be obtained in what can only be described as sheet form. As such they are called hand pads, the sponge centre being thin enough and flexible enough to make them particularly suitable for use on curved surfaces. As well as rectangular sheets it is also possible to obtain these in circular form. An advantage of these thinner sheets is that they can be cut to shape to enable work to be carried out in areas that would otherwise be inaccessible.

Sanding disks

The term sanding disk is one that is loosely applied to flexible abrasive disks of many types and they are available in a wide range of materials and grades. Better quality ones have a pressed fibre backing

rather than paper or cloth, which gives a greater strength and longer life. They are frequently used with portable drills, where their high speed and rapid rotation enables a good rate of metal or wood removal. While at one time it was usual for them to be held in place on a mandrel with a couple of large washers and a screw or nut, the modern way is to stick them to the pad with an adhesive that remains flexible enough to allow them to be removed after use. They are often used in miniature drills for delicate work and as a rule in that case will be permanently stuck to a backing which is held to a mandrel with some form of screw. The one big drawback with the use of sanding disks is the difficulty of preventing the edges from digging into the work. This means that frequently the finish obtained will have a series of circular marks that are difficult to remove.

Sanding strips

Abrasive cloth is also available in strip form, which is a very useful way in which to use it. There are a number of grades and different materials available in this form

A cartridge roll consists of a roll of abrasive cloth that fits over a sponge rubber pad, itself secured to a mandrel. These are available ia a large range of sizes and grits and are designed to be used in a hand held power drill.

Tapered cartridge rolls like these are available in a variety of grits. Because of the way they are manufactured the rolls replenish themselves, new grit coming through as the top layer is exhausted.

and it is also possible to get it in various widths. The most popular of these is one inch or 25mm. The advantage of using the strips is that general access to the area that is being worked on is made easier and there is less waste. Being cloth-backed, the strips are extremely durable and well worth considering as an alternative to sheet material. Strip material can either be obtained in short lengths or

on a roll, in which case the length required for a particular purpose is cut off.

Sanding bands

Sanding bands are strips of abrasive cloth designed to fit over a sponge rubber mandrel, which gives the material great flexibility. They are particularly useful for working on curved surfaces and can be obtained in a variety of diameters. The size

Unlike the normal cartridge roll which fits on to a sponge rubber pad, the tapered type require a special mandrel that fits directly inside them.

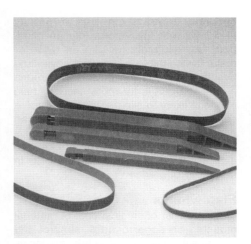

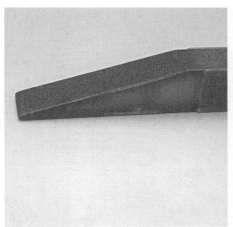

These are bands for sanding sticks, together with their holders. Bands and holders are available in several sizes; the bands in a variety of grits. They are convenient for working on flat surfaces and in small area.

A view of a sanding stick, complete with an abrasive band. The shape of the stick gives it considerable versatility and large ones when fitted with very fine abrasives are suitable replacements for the old fashioned buffing stick.

of the mandrel will vary according to the size of the band.

Cartridge rolls

Sanding bands usually have a butt or lap joint, but cartridge rolls consist of a roll of material in the form of a spiral. They are usually of a small diameter and are favoured by toolmakers for die grinding, a high precision operation. As the small

portable drills are very similar in size and shape to the professional quality die grinding tool; readers will not be surprised to find that they are also favoured for use on these little machines as well. They can be obtained either as straightforward circular rolls or in the form of a taper that allows the operator to work in very confined areas. A special mandrel is required in order to be able to use the tapered form.

The band is held on to a sanding stick with a spring loaded section that keeps the band reasonably tight. It also allows the band to be slid round the stick when a section of it becomes worn, thus allowing a new section to be taken into use.

A flap wheel. As with most other products of the type, they are available in differing sizes and grits and designed mainly for use in powered hand drills. Flap wheels have a high rate of material removal and adapt themselves particularly well to curved surfaces.

Sanding sticks

A more modern version of the buffing stick is known as a sanding stick and is a wedge-shaped spring loaded tool over which is slipped an abrasive belt of the appropriate diameter and width. As usual these are available in a number of different grades. The advantage of the system is that it enables operations to be carried out in areas that otherwise would be very difficult to deal with. Although almost

certainly the system was originally designed with the woodworker in mind, belts are available for use on wood or metal. Using these is a distinct advantage over the idea of folding the abrasive around a file - the belt is far more securely held and less likely to slip. In addition, when a section of the belt becomes worn it can easily be moved around the stick and a fresh section used. The sticks are available in several sizes and the belts in a number of grades.

Flap wheels

These consist of small sheets of material mounted on edge round a mandrel and are available in a wide variety of grades as well as various diameters and thicknesses of wheel. Mainly they are used in a portable electric drill and are highly suited to the high number of revolutions at which these machines rotate. With care, flap wheels can be used to remove metal in places that are not accessible when sheet material is used. There is one problem and that is the fact that in use they do tend to snatch at the metal and this can cause unwanted damage. It is therefore advisable to secure the work to a bench and hold the drill with two hands to prevent this from happening. An alternative is to mount the drill in a stand and hold the work in one's hand when presenting it to the flap wheel. It is necessary to take care when doing this as a lot of heat is generated and it is all too easy to burn oneself.

Chapter Four

Belt and Disk Sanders

Belt sanders consist of a pair of rollers with a continuous belt forming a loop of abrasive cloth running round them. A slight radius on the rollers ensures that the belt

remains in position during operations. One side of the loop runs over a flat metal section, the length of which depends on the type of machine. Work is carried out by presenting the metal to the rotating band and by applying pressure where the belt runs over the flat piece. The rate of metal removal depends on the coarseness of the belt, the speed of rotation and the pressure applied. In order to drive the machine it is common practice to use a motor with an extended shaft as the axle of one roller. On larger machines it is more likely that one of the rollers will be belt driven.

The value of belt sanders in the engineering workshop should not be underestimated. While generally thought of as a means of polishing, by careful selection of the type of machine and grade of belt they can also be used for shaping

A large industrial bed-belt sander. Smaller versions are available that are suitable for the home workshop.

A vertical narrow band machine in use. Note the use of heatproof gloves and safety glasses by the operator.

purposes. When using a coarse belt the machines are capable of rapid removal of metal, but care is necessary otherwise it is possible to remove too much. In addition it is all too easy to remove metal from the wrong place by merely applying a little too much pressure on one side.

Horizontal machines

Most, if not all, horizontal belt sanders will use a fairly wide belt and therefore are best suited for work on flat surfaces and possibly outside radii. As with either type of machine if a coarse belt is used a good rate of metal removal is available. However, it requires care in order to avoid the metal removal coming from the wrong place. Horizontal machines are popular for use in home workshops but we must not forget that they also have a place in industry where it is not unusual to find machines that use belts 300 mm or more in width.

Vertical machines

Machines that have the belt operating in a vertical position as a rule are used for different purposes to those using a horizontal belt and more often than not use a narrower belt. While the horizontal machine is almost always used to generate flat surfaces the vertical type is frequently used for shaping objects as well as for polishing purposes. The vertical machine otherwise works on the same principle as the horizontal type with the belt

A wide belt vertical machine as used in industry. Rapid removal of metal is possible using a machine such as this.

38

rotating on rollers and following a flat bed, which in this case consists of a narrow flat metal strip. In addition they have a table on which the work is rested while it is pushed against the belt. In most instances the table will be adjustable, enabling it to be set not only at ninety degrees to the belt but also at an obtuse angle. The precise angle can be set quite accurately with a protractor making the machine extremely useful for work where a precise angle is required.

Multi-purpose machines

Some of the machines designed for use in small workshops are adaptable for horizontal or vertical operations and frequently this usually also means that the belt can be set at an obtuse angle, making them very versatile machines. However, as a rule multi functional machines such as these use a wider belt than those designed purely for vertical operation, which means that they do not have quite the same versatility when it comes to working on objects that are of an awkward shape.

Disk sanding machines

Disk Sanding machines work on a different principle to belt sanders and as the name suggests the disk sander consists of a flat disk to which the abrasive paper or cloth is stuck. This has to be done with an adhesive that is easily removable to allow for the abrasive disks to be replaced. It is essential when putting the abrasive disk in position that the whole of it is stuck firmly to the metal disk as well as ensuring that it is lined up accurately with the disk edges. Failure to do this can have two results. Firstly the disk will in all probability not

An old industrial machine with a horizontal belt and disk.

A machine designed with the small workshop in mind. The vertical band is set at an angle. Frequently this type of machine also includes a sanding disk at one side.

create the flat surface that is required. A bumping effect will be created by the air in the space where there is no adhesive and will cause ridges in the work. Secondly and again because of the air space

The upright flat plate of the vertical machine shown earlier has been replaced with a round bar, making it possible to fit a very narrow belt for making internal radii.

This photograph shows how a narrow band (actually a normal one cut down the centre) has been fitted over the round bar seen in the previous photograph. It is now possible to shape internal radii using the machine.

between abrasive and metal disk, there is every chance that the abrasive disk will tear during operations. Apart from the annoyance of having to change the disk, on large machines it can also be very dangerous as there is every chance it will snatch the work and damage it.

The disk sander normally has a table on which the work is rested, which will usually be adjustable to allow work to be done at an angle. Some machines include a fence that allows work to be set at an angle across the face of the table. This acts as a very useful guide as well as giving added support to the work.

Also available are machines that combine the best of both worlds using both a belt and a disk. The belt may be vertical or horizontal and both belt and disk have all the adjustable features one expects from a single unit machine. Both abrasives are driven from a single motor making a space saving machine as well as an economical one.

Use of belt and disk sanders

Apart from the more usual grinding and polishing operations these machines are useful for shaping work. It is possible to set work at an angle and by using a rolling motion against a sanding disk it is quite possible to create a radius or even a compound radius if one so requires. They can be used for chamfering edges and of course the removal of burrs. It is possible to use vertical machines having narrow abrasive bands for precise forming of internal radii. A normal band is split in two lengthways around its whole circumference, making two narrow bands. The normal flat supporting bar is replaced with a round bar of slightly under the diameter required and is used as a guide for the extra narrow belt. This arrangement is very useful. In particular, the use of a very fine grade belt allows for polishing of items when using any other method is extremely difficult.

It is possible to obtain small hand held belt sanders in a variety of sizes; they look similar to the hand held pistol type drill, but instead of a chuck have an extended section driving a small belt. Mainly aimed at the building and DIY market these little machines are worth considering for engineering work, not for generating flat surfaces but for shaping purposes. By using one of them it is possible to hold the work securely in a vice and this allows for greater accuracy.

Use of guides and jigs

All these types of machines can be used with belts or disks of varying grades of grit and in some instances such as the smaller disk type machines it is also possible to obtain disks using diamonds. These have the advantage of not needing replacement anywhere near as often as the more convention type of disk. No matter what the grade of abrasive, all the machines are capable of ruining work as well as doing a good job. A second or two of inattention is sufficient for too much

metal to be removed, or for metal to be removed from the wrong place. A way of lessening this possibility is to improvise guides and jigs of some sort or another. Some of the machines such as the horizontal belt sander and the disk sander will possibly have a basic form of guide, to allow work to be done at roughly ninety degrees to the face of the belt, in the case of a disk sander it is even a possibility that there will be some sort of angular guide. As a general rule these are not as accurate as one would wish and will have to be treated with caution. Far better to make a check with a square or protractor rather than going ahead and then discovering that the guide is not as accurate as one would like.

Simple guides can easily be improvised. For example, if a piece of bar is bolted on the table of a vertical machine at exactly ninety degrees to the face of the belt, it will be reasonable to anticipate that the work will also be at ninety degrees. Likewise to make a radius, a simple piece of plate with a pin fitted in it will do the job adequately. It is just a case of measuring from the centre of the pin to the face of the belt, clamping the plate at the correct distance and using that to do the job.

Tool sharpening

The subject of tool sharpening is dealt with in greater depth elsewhere in the book, but it is worth remembering that all belt and disk sanders do an excellent job when used to sharpen tools. Lathe tools are comparatively easy to do by hand, although again some people might prefer to use some sort of guide. A piece of strip steel bolted to the table at the angle required will work well enough and it is just a case of changing the angle in order to sharpen the required faces of the tool.

The normal type of drill grinding jig can be clamped to the table of either a horizontal belt, or disk sander and there isno need to worry about the height of the drill point as anywhere on the flat belt will do. Sharpening of large drills can rarely be done in a jig and for these the sanding machine is ideal as there is generally a far better chance of seeing what one is doing than there is when bending over an off hand grinder.

A word of caution though; work done on a sanding machine will get just as hot, if not hotter than that done on a grindstone, so remember to keep it cool.

Operation of machines

The general safety rules, such as the use of safety glasses, gloves, etc that are The dust is made up of a mixture of abrasive grains, metal and dirt, plus a few bits of material from the belt or disk thrown in. It is highly toxic and breathing it must be avoided at all cost.

Not only is the residue extremely toxic, the dust is also very abrasive. Care must therefore be taken to ensure that it is kept well away from the bearing surfaces of any machinery. As well as operating as far away from machines as possible it is advisable to cover any machines while grinding operations are going on. There is extra need to cover oneself, as the dust is very difficult to remove from clothing. It is usual in industry for anyone engaged in these sorts of operations to wear a leather apron; in the home workshop this can be substituted with a plastic one. In industry there would be a form of extraction system that would take the dust well away from the working area. It is not really practical to make such a system for the small workshop, but there is nothing to prevent the vacuum cleaner being used while such work is carried out. It can either be held by a willing volunteer, if you can find such a person, or the nozzle could be tied in someway in such a position that it will do the job.

Good stout gloves are also advisable. If one does happen to catch a finger on a revolving sanding device it will result in the painful removal of skin and the use of stout gloves can prevent this from happening. Gloves should not be made of any form of plastic as the heat generated can melt most plastics, which results in burns to the flesh.

Chapter Five

The Off Hand Grinder

The normal double ended grinding machine found in the average workshop is called an off hand grinder and is no doubt the grinding machine that will be the one that is most familiar to all readers. It is one of the most used machines in a workshop and also one of the most misused. This is probably best described using the words written by the late Edgar Westbury many years ago.

"It is an indispensable tool in every engineering workshop and may, with intelligent use, be applied to a very wide range of work with reasonable efficiency, but it must be confessed that it is more often abused than properly used. Wheels of incorrect specification run at incorrect speeds and grossly overloaded, are all too common, even in machine shops, quite efficiently organised in other respects. For these sins the blame must be laid on the users of the machines, as their makers have done everything possible to ensure their efficient performance and the modern examples of tool grinders, however simple in form, have very carefully designed and constructed bearings and spindles and provisions for efficient drive."

Off hand machines can be bought as stand alone versions, in which case they come complete on a pedestal base, or they can be obtained for use on a bench. There are instances where both parts can be purchased separately thus allowing a person who has bought one for bench mounting and subsequently wishing to mount it on a pedestal can do so. The grinding machine should always be firmly bolted down. In the case of the pedestal grinder, the pedestal should be secured to the floor using bolts of as large a diameter as possible. The bench-mounted machine should be bolted firmly to a bench that has a good stout top and bolts should pass through the top and be secured with nuts and washers. It is not sufficient to screw it to a bench using wood screws. In small workshops there may not be sufficient space to allow the machine to have a permanent position, it will therefore be necessary to arrange things in such a way that it can be fastened securely in position when required and can be put away when not in use. It is realised that in the case of people who use a temporary space as a workshop even this arrangement is not easy and one way of solving the problem is to mount the

A typical offhand grinder. This one accepts six-inch diameter wheels. One of the most common tools in any workshop but also possibly the most misused and misunderstood.

machine on a piece of board, such as chipboard or medium density fibreboard, which can then be clamped firmly to the worktop when the machine is to be used. Using an off hand grinder resting loose on a bench or other surface while it is in use is a very dangerous practice and should be avoided at all costs. The fast revolving shaft will create vibration that will cause the machine to move around the bench and any uneven balance of the wheel will make matters much worse.

It is possible to obtain machines in all sizes, the size being largely governed by the diameter of the wheel. Choice of size

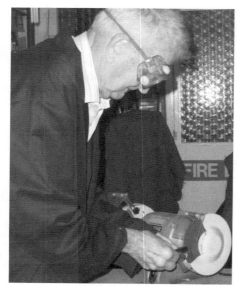

The offhand grinder in use. Note the operator using safety glasses; gloves are not in use. If the tool gets too hot, the temper of it can be impaired. Using the bare hand ensures that a change of temperature can be felt and the tool left to cool down. Some people may feel it safer to use a glove, in which case the tool should be frequently withdrawn.

44

will depend on personal circumstances such as space and cost. As a rule it is best to buy as large a grinder as possible; it is also advisable to purchase a good quality model. Most off hand grinders work simply by using a double-ended spindle that is an extension to the shaft in an electric motor. In the case of good quality ones the shaft will run in ball races, thus giving a smooth running wheel. It also means the shaft is less prone to wear than is the case where the shaft is in plain bearings. Ideally all bearings whether plain or otherwise should have a shield to prevent grinding dust from entering. In many instances this will take the form of a metal cover with a soft washer that is in contact with the shaft. From time to time the cover and washer should be removed. If possible, the soft washer should be replaced but if for some reason this is not practical it must be thoroughly cleaned to remove all traces of grinding dust.

Safety shields

Each wheel should have a transparent safety cover. In the case of older machines this will most likely be made of specially strengthened glass and held in place with a metal frame. Many less expensive grinders have the shield made of Perspex or a similar transparent plastic and as far as safety is concerned there is no objection to the use of this material - in fact in some ways it may even be preferable as glass shields are generally supported round the edges with a metal frame, which can create a blind spot when working. The plastic shield is unlikely to have this edge to the shield so the blind spot does not exist. The shield must be adjustable in order that the best position can be found for each task to be undertaken as well as for it to be comfortable for every user.

Plastic shields tend to get scratched and discoloured as a result of the grinding dust, in the event of this happening the transparency can sometimes be restored by using one of the proprietary scratch removing pastes sold for use on motor vehicles. Another alternative is the replacement of the plastic, which is usually a comparatively easy task as most are only held in position with nuts and bolts and suitable plastic is readily available. Should a shield need replacing as a matter of urgency, perhaps because of it breaking, it is possible to use a piece of one of the transparent cases that hold compact disks and are known as jewel cases, as a temporary measure. Glass shields are much less prone to these problems but they too can be restored with rubbing compounds.

Grinding rests

Each wheel should have a suitable rest to support the tool and the better the quality of the rest the easier it will be to obtain a good result when grinding tools. The rests must be adjustable in order to allow the tool to be set at the required angle and when setting the rest to the required angle it is essential to ensure the adjusting bolts are tightened thoroughly to prevent it slipping out of position when in use. If not properly tightened, rests have a nasty habit of moving very slowly in such a way that the movement is not readily noticeable with the result that the wrong angle is put on the tool.

Tool rests should be substantial items and if designed to go partially round the side of the wheel as well as across the periphery, so much the better. Unfortunately

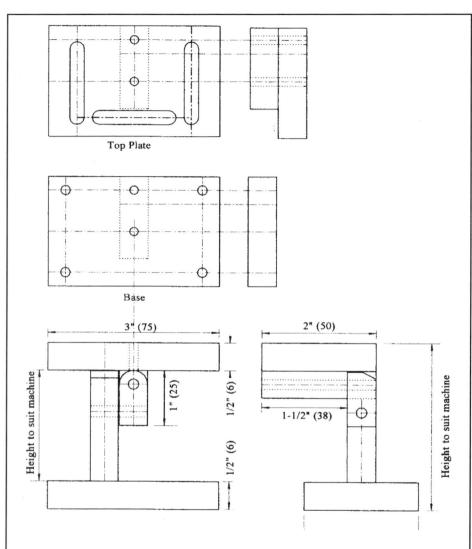

Top Plate

Base

3" (75)

2" (50)

Height to suit machine

1" (25)

1/2" (6)

1/2" (6)

1-1/2" (38)

Height to suit machine

Suggested design for a substantial tool rest. Note these are not construction drawings but only for guidance as all machines vary

when a grinder is first purchased many have small, flimsy and unsuitable rests. Some are fitted with small rests that are nothing more that a piece of sheet metal folded to shape. Generally not only will this be too small but also it is unlikely to be accurate. The top face will quite probably have a slight curve making it impossible to place the tool accurately in position. A rest of this type should be replaced, as good workmanship will never result from its use. It must be remembered that the off-hand grinder used correctly is a precision tool and therefore accessories should always be of a high quality.

It is quite easy to make a new rest and it can be fabricated from mild steel. When doing so it is advisable to make the table part from a good solid piece of mild steel plate that will give plenty of support to the tool. As well as basic tool rests it is also possible to make simple attachments that ensure that the correct angles are ground on tools.

Whatever type of rest is used it has to be adjusted so that it is as close to the wheel as possible, without actually

rubbing on it, in order to prevent the material being ground catching between the wheel and rest, something that could result in wheel failure and a possible accident to the operator

It is usually recommended that when grinding tools only the periphery of the wheel should be used, as pressure

A grinder designed with the woodworker in mind. It has one wheel and on the other side an abrasive band. It also revolves at a slower rate that those designed for sharpening metalworking tools. Above the grinding wheel there is an attachment to assist in sharpening chisels and plane irons.

that it will not weaken the wheel in any way. For example a sharp pointed tool used with pressure for a period of time will make a groove that will cause a weakness. This could ultimately cause the wheel to break up when in use and therefore should be avoided at all costs. If it is found necessary to use the side of the wheel do so as close to the periphery as possible, the nearer to the centre that wear is created the weaker the wheel will become.

applied there is applied at the strongest part. While this is the ideal way to use the wheel, it is not always practical to do so and at times there is little choice but to use the side. If it is necessary to do so, care must be taken to do it in such a way

When tools are being ground to shape, or sometimes even when sharpened on a grinder, the material will absorb a considerable amount of heat. Under no circumstances should the area that has

This rather unusual grinder is something of a cross between an offhand grinder and a tool and cutter grinder. It has two large adjustable tables designed to be set at the angle required. They are slotted to accept any fittings that may be required. The wheels used are considerably thicker than those normally used for offhand grinding, presumably because the machine is designed so that work is carried out on the side of the wheel rather than the periphery.

been ground be touched by hand until the object has had time to cool. It is frequently the practice to cool work with water between times when it is presented to the grinding wheel. There is nothing generally wrong with this approach except that it is possible in doing so to cause the metal to become too hard and brittle, or alternatively the hardness can be reduced by changing the temper. It should never of course ever be allowed to get red hot, but these things do happen and if, when it is in that state it is put into water hardening may result and completely change the temper of the tool. It is necessary therefore to make sure the tool does not get that hot in the first place.

Positioning the machine

Because of the dust created by the grinding operation the off-hand grinder should be placed as far away from machinery as possible and if it is possible to organise a means of extracting the dust, so much the better. Frequently a special small area shielded from the main workshop is used and if that can be arranged we have the perfect situation. Good lighting is essential and on some machines a light will be fitted, otherwise an adjustable lamp that can be arranged to shine a light directly on the work can be used.

Using the machine

Most of the necessities when using the machine such as not allowing too much heat to be generated and using the wheel only for working on the material it is intended for have already been covered. There must be a good firm grip on the work and it is essential to ensure that one has a firm footing. It is also advisable to ask other people who may be present in the workshop to stand away during operations; there are several reasons for doing so. Firstly they might cause a distraction and not giving the work ones full attention can end up with spoiled work, a damaged wheel or worse still, injury to one or other of those people. The operator should be wearing suitable protective items, which at the very least should be a facemask, eye shield and possibly gloves. A bystander is unlikely to have the same protection and therefore is vulnerable not only to dust but also in danger from any particles that fly off the stone.

From time to time when using an offhand grinder, it will be found that the wheel is no longer doing its job properly. Often the cause of this is the fact that the wheel has glazed over or become shiny. Sometimes this may be because it has been used to grind soft metal, something for which it is definitely not suited. While a hardened and tempered tool will clear the surface of the wheel, softer metals just gradually blunt the grains, without removing them thus glazing the wheel. The best tool for dealing with soft metals is a sander and the temptation to use the grinder must be avoided

Tool and cutter grinders

The off hand grinder is frequently used to sharpen items such as lathe tools and usually the work is carried out freehand. The best machine to use for this is a tool and cutter grinder, a name that speaks for itself, however although possession of these machines appears to be on the increase, they are still comparatively rare items in the home workshop. As far as sharpening milling cutters, whether for horizontal or vertical machines, is

A photograph of a typical cutter grinder. In the foreground is the tool holder. The view of the diamond coated cup wheel shows clearly how it is possible to work on the periphery.

Another view of the same tool and cutter grinder. On the left can be seen the collet that holds end mills and slot drills in place.

concerned then for ease of so doing a tool and cutter grinder is a necessity. This is not to say that some enterprising people have not managed to do the job using the off hand grinder by making special adapters for the work. Those who do manage it will most certainly require a substantial rest for the machine in order to get the required adjustment and in order to support the special holders required.

The reasons why we do not find more tool and cutter grinders in small workshops are two fold. Firstly they are very expensive to buy and secondly quite difficult to make, although there are some excellent plans available for anyone wishing to have a go at doing so. Basically the grinder has many similarities to the off hand grinder with the spindle that holds the wheel generally running horizontally. There the similarity ends as instead of a rest or table the cutter grinder has an arrangement to accept collets to hold the cutter. The holder must be able to move in at least three planes - horizontally, vertically and to a required angle. The first two of these will usually be done by means of lead screws, the pitch of which must be very fine in order to allow the minute adjustment required, a variety of arrangements are used for the angular or rotary movement. More sophisticated machines will allow the user to grind the spiral edges as well as the end teeth. An improvised but useful device can consist

This is an example of a Quorn Tool and Cutter Grinder, designed by the late Professor Chaddock as a project for model engineers. It is a very versatile machine and numerous examples have been made.

of a l web of the cutter and then pushing it along. Because of the peg the spiral must rotate along its natural axis and if during that movement the cutter happens to be in contact with a grindstone the edge will be sharpened. The adjustment required to do this and at the same time for the cutter to remain near to its true diameter is very fine indeed.

A number of ideas have been published that allow the end teeth of a cutter to be sharpened. They generally involve setting the cutter in a hole in a of a length of square bar, which is used as an indexing device, hexagonal material being used for three flute cutters. The holders are then pushed along a heavy rest such as the one shown, using a screw adjustment at the rear of the holder in order to ensure each tooth is

This machine is mounted with a wheel designed purely for sharpening cutters for engraving.

ground to exactly the same depth.

Gear Grinding

The process of gear grinding is in some ways similar to that of cutter grinding. Most gear wheels are not ground at all instead

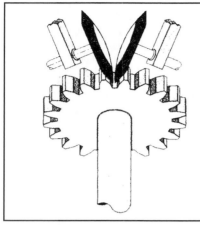

The advantage of grinding gears to shape is that a more accurate profile and smoother finish can be obtained. The illustration shows how two specially shaped wheels form both sides of a tooth

they are used as machined; however some are machined and then given a ground finish. The advantage of gears that have been ground is that they will not only mesh together more efficiently than plain machined ones, but will also be much quieter in operation. One only has to hear a traction engine in action to find out just how noisy gears can be, most of the gears used in that case are plain cast iron, possibly dressed with a hand grinder, but certainly not accurately machined and the noise created is tremendous

It is rare indeed that model engineers will grind gears as generally a special machine is used; this has two rotating spindles running in unison, each fitted with specially shaped grinding wheels. The shape will depend on the shape of the teeth of the gear and in turn this will depend on its pitch circle diameter. The machines require very careful and accurate adjustment in order to ensure absolute precision.

Sometimes gears are ground using a single grinding wheel, specially shaped to the format of the gap between the teeth

of the gear. In that case a machine similar to a cutter grinder is used. It is essential that a good supply of coolant be used when carrying out this type of operation as the fact that both sides of the wheel are being used means that extra heat is being generated. The wheels used are specially bonded and under no circumstances should any attempt be made to dress a normal grinding wheel to shape for the purpose. This will only result in a weakened wheel that will be in danger of breaking up in use.

Finally

The off-hand grinder is a valuable tool and successful machining depends not only on the skill of the machinist but also on how well he or she is able to keep an edge on the tools. To be successful it is necessary to treat the grinder with the same care as one would a lathe or milling machine. Doing this will repay one's efforts a hundred fold; misuse it and the fact that it has been misused will be reflected in all other aspects of the workmanship.

Chapter Six

Portable Grinding Tools

Grinding operations on the whole do not lend themselves to work with portable tools. It is difficult in most cases to hold a tool steady enough for any degree of accuracy to be achieved, therefore in the majority of instances work with portable tools will be confined to such tasks as grinding off excess welding material deburring and similar functions. In many cases these jobs can only be done with portable tools as the work is too large or too heavy to be taken to a machine.

Angle grinders

The angle grinder is quite a versatile tool and is generally available in two sizes. The tool in most cases consists of a powerful electric motor housed in a plastic body. The spindle of the motor is fitted with bevel gears, the final drive therefore is at ninety degrees to the motor shaft and it is designed to accept a flat abrasive disk which is made specially for this sort of work. Disks are available in a variety of grades that are mainly designed for use

A typical angle grinder of which there are numerous examples available on the market.

on certain materials and are designated for use on brick and concrete with some types designed for use on metal. This of course is the type with which this book is mainly concerned.

Using an angle grinder is something of an acquired art and very much a personalised skill. Most people seem to develop their own personal technique. Certain rules do apply however; for example, the grinder should always be kept moving along the work and many people like to use the disk at an angle. When truing up a weld it is common for the edge of the wheel to be used but again various people have different ideas on the matter.

Another use for an angle grinder is to cut metal to size something at which it is very effective. The wheel can be driven straight into the work at a ninety-degree angle and although because of the width of the wheel there is some waste of material cutting operations can be carried out very quickly. When the angle grinder is used in this way the action is similar to that of a cut off saw that also uses a wheel.

All wheels designed for angle grinders have details of their type and uses printed on them and they should only be used for that purpose.

For heavy-duty work, particularly in a situation in the open air, the angle grinder is a very useful tool, but by its very nature when using it a great deal of care is required. It is essential to wear safety glasses and advisable to also wear heavy-duty gloves. It is also essential that bystanders are kept clear. The tool causes tiny particles of the material being worked on, as well as similar particles from the wheel to be thrown a considerable distance away from the actual working area. This can be dangerous to the unwary. The safety guards that are fitted have a very limited ability to prevent a spray of grinding dust.

Power drills

The DIY type of hand held power drill, as well as the battery-powered version can be used for various grinding and sanding purposes. Accessories are available that enable sanding disks to be fitted and small stones ready mounted on mandrels, known as grinding points, that have already been mentioned are available. It is best to avoid the use of grinding wheels of a large diameters as the chucks supplied with these drills are not designed to cope with the type of strain imposed by using grinding wheels and there could be a tendency for the wheel to work loose. Although the available sanding disks and their fittings being flexible do not impose quite the same strain as a mounted wheel of large diameter. In spite of these problems, points and sanding disks can be used very effectively for certain tasks.

A mini drill. Like the angle grinder there are numerous examples available; some are mains powered and others work on low voltages. They are very versatile and ideal for small work and much in demand by model makers.

Where this type of drill comes into its own is for polishing, various cloth mops are available that are similar to those used on a fixed shaft, except that in this case they have to be held in place with a nut rather than the mandrel having a threaded end. The advantage of using them is that the drill can be used at an angle and polish into areas that are difficult when using a fixed set up. The use of an eye shield when doing this sort of work is essential, as pieces tend to fly off the mops and could cause injury even if they are soft.

Mini drills

For small jobs the mini drill is an ideal tool and is a delight to use, there is a wide variety of them available, some work from mains electricity, others are driven by batteries that as a rule are rechargeable. Because they are small they are much easier to operate than the angle grinder, although the rate of metal removal is far less.

There is a wide variety of grinding and polishing materials available for use with the drills; most of these are small grinding points that can be held in the drill by a small chuck. There does not appear to be a great deal of variety in the type of grit that are available, but it is possible to obtain the points in various degrees of coarseness.

The tools are very useful for making minor adjustments to work and are popular with craftsmen engaged in such tasks as die making, the small size giving access to areas that would be more difficult to work on with larger tools.

As well as small grindstones it is possible to obtain a variety of sanding disks of various types and in differing grades and these are very good for polishing purposes. In addition, polishing mops are also available for giving the work that final finish and they work very well with a fine grinding medium such as metal polish.

With all portable tools there is an operating problem because the accuracy of use depends entirely on the ability of the operator to hold the tool steady. It is

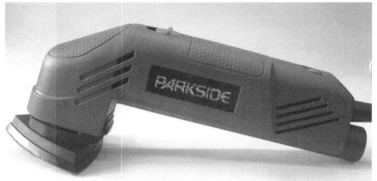

A detail sander, one of a number of various types of sander designed basically with woodworkers in mind. However, this type can be quite useful for some metal working operations.

therefore best if some form of support can be used. It is surprising the difference leaning ones arm against a table or wall can make this being sufficient to stop the tool from wavering around.

Sheet sanders

The sheet sander is likely to be used more by the woodworker than those working with metal. The machine has a flat semi-flexible plate that is covered with a replaceable abrasive sheet of abrasive material. These sheets are available in a variety of grits as

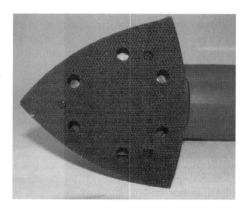

dedicated replacements or they can be cut from a normal sheet of material. The advantage of this type of tool is that it is possible to obtain a decent flat finish on a piece of work, without the effort of using a sanding block by hand. The tools can be obtained with motors of various power specifications, including in some instances rechargeable ones.

Sheet palm sanders

Similar in many ways to the sheet sander, the sheet palm sander has a smaller sanding plate and therefore accepts smaller sanding sheets. Unlike the sheet sander that has a handle for the operator to use, the palm sander is designed to be pressed to the work with the palm of the hand. This allows greater pressure to be applied and allows more rapid removal of material.

Corner and detail sanders

The detail sander works in a similar

The underside of the pad of the detail sander. Special abrasive sheets that stick directly to the pads are used.

One of the abrasive sheets designed to fit the detail sander.

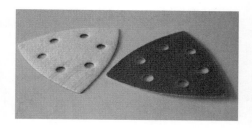

fashion to the sheet sander, but instead of holding rectangular abrasive sheets, the sheets are of a triangular pattern. They are secured with some form of adhesive; the exact method will vary depending on the manufacturer of the tool. As the name suggests, the smaller and differently shaped abrasive sheets make them useful for cleaning up odd shaped work. The tools are available in a variety of sizes and the miniature ones are particularly useful for metal working purposes. The so-called corner sander is generally larger than the detail sander but is otherwise more or less identical to the detail sander and does exactly the same job.

Random orbital sanders

This type of sander in many ways reverts to the idea of using a rotating disk on a hand drill, as the abrasive disks used are a very similar shape. There the similarity ends however, as the tools are designed to have pressure applied over the top of the disk. The extra pressure means that there can be more rapid removal of material and is also an aid to accuracy in use.

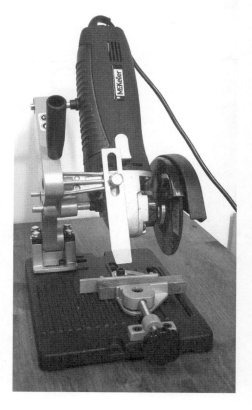

A stand like this allows an angle grinder to be used as a cut off tool. It is essential when doing so that the correct type of cutting disk is fitted; under no circumstances may a disk designed for grinding be used for cutting.

Chapter Seven

Surface Grinding Machines

Of all the various forms of mechanical grinding, surface grinding is arguably the most common and the process is used for both obtaining perfect accuracy and producing a very fine finish. A surface-grinding machine operates in many ways similar to a milling machine, although there are major differences in the way the two types of machine are constructed. Instead of a mandrel that accepts collets for milling cutters there is a spindle to hold the grinding wheel, which can be raised and lowered or as is more likely the compound table of the machine can be raised or lowered in much the same way as the milling machine. The compound table is similar to that of the miller but with a mechanism allowing the table to travel faster than the lead screw found on the latter. Nevertheless it could be said that the same general principals apply to

A typical surface grinding machine.

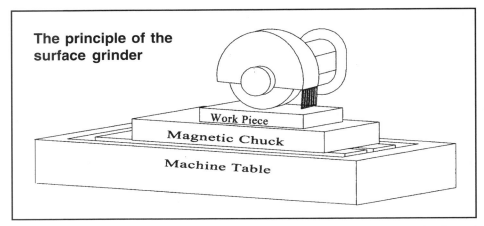

The principle of the surface grinder

Work Piece

Magnetic Chuck

Machine Table

surface grinding in as much as the work is passed under the tool by means of having it secured to the moveable table. In the case of the grinder the tool is a grindstone, instead of a milling cutter. Also the rate of travel of the work is usually considerably faster than is the case when

milling and of necessity the depth of metal that is removed is far less than can be achieved with a milling cutter. As with milling machines in some types the traverse of the table is carried out under power. Other machines are designed purely for hand operation and instead of a handle to create the movement a lever is used.

Magnetic chucks
When working on steel or iron, usually the work will be held to the table with a magnetic chuck, this being the name applied to what amounts to an oversized non permanent magnet. Because the wheel is pressing down there is the possibility of work flexing unless fully supported underneath and magnetic chucks are flat in construction and long enough to support the work throughout its length, thus preventing any flexing, as well as holding it secure.

A small surface grinder designed for standing on a normal bench and ideal for the home workshop. At one time these were quite popular; now they are rarely seen.

A close up picture showing the magnetic chuck, the most usual means of securing work on a surface grinder.

Securing work with adhesives

Large magnetic chucks are very expensive items and for the model engineer working at home the expense of buying one can be saved when securing the work by sticking it down with double-sided adhesive tape. The type of tape sold for holding down carpets is ideal for the purpose. It is necessary for there to be adequate flat surfaces on the component to be machined, in order that the tape will hold the work secure. It is also necessary to ensure that both the component and the table are absolutely free from oil and grease otherwise the piece is likely to move. For degreasing it is best to purchase a proper degreasing solution; nowadays these are generally available in spray type containers. They are available from good tool suppliers but it is often far less expensive to use one of those sold for household purposes, although it must be designated purely for degreasing rather than one designed for general domestic cleaning.

To remove the component from the table a sharp sideways blow with a heavy non-metallic mallet is all that is needed and it will come away easily. It is also possible to hold work to the table with cyanoacrylate adhesive (Super Glue). Again both surfaces must be thoroughly degreased and the adhesive given time to completely dry. A smart sideways tap will also release work held to the table using this method.

Of course there is also nothing whatever to prevent the work being held in a normal machine vice, bolted securely to the table.

It is also essential to keep the piece being ground clear of any raised sections that might create an obstruction. Not only would this prevent the wheel passing over the work but also there is a chance that if the side of the wheel was to catch the obstruction, the wheel might break if it is brought with any force against it. Unless for some reason it is not possible to do so, grinding operations must be completed in one sweep of the wheel and this will largely decide the position on the

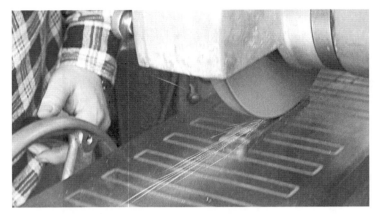

The surface grinder in use, showing how the work piece is retained entirely by the magnetic chuck.

table at which the work will be mounted. It is virtually impossible to grind a length of material in two sections without leaving a witness mark. In the event that the operation cannot be done in one sweep it might well be necessary to resort to scraping in order to marry the two machined faces and to remove the inevitable minute lip caused by having to take the second sweep.

Types of grinder

There are two types of surface grinder, vertical and horizontal, in the same way that there are two types of milling machine. The horizontal machine is the most common and the grinding wheel is mounted on a spindle driven by a motor in much the same fashion as the milling cutter. However, while a cutter for a horizontal miller has to be supported via an overhead arm, this is not so in the case of the grinding wheel. Plain wheels are used and they are mounted on the spindle against a back plate; support for the other side of the wheel is similar to that used on the off-hand grinder, with a large washer

applying pressure to the weakest part of the wheel. Usually only the periphery of the wheel is used and it is necessary to ensure that it is in good condition with the periphery at exactly ninety degrees to the sides, in order to get good results.

This means that it is necessary to keep the wheel properly dressed and to do this some machines have a position to fit a diamond dresser in the cover above the wheel. When required this can be brought into contact and moved across the wheel, because it is fitted in this way absolute accuracy is ensured. The other method is to have a single point tool in a steel holder that is fitted on the machine table. Usually this will simply be by holding it in place with the magnets. The dressing tool is at an angle of about thirty degrees from the horizontal and by traversing the wheel across it we again have the situation where a perfect alignment across the wheel ensures absolute accuracy.

Machines that have the spindle vertical use wheels that are cylindrical or cupped sometimes referred to as coned or dished. This type of machine has the advantage

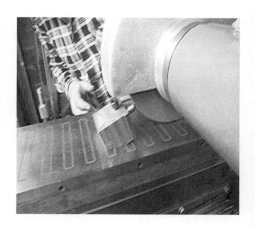

Dressing the wheel of a surface grinder, using a single point diamond mounted in a block on the magnetic chuck. The grainy effect of the photograph is actually particles flying from the wheel as the dressing tool does its work. It is a job that really calls for the use of a face mask as well as safety glasses.

that a rotary table can be used more easily and there are examples of vertical spindled machines that have a rotary table fitted instead of the more normal type. There are similar arrangements for dressing the wheels.

The wheels used for surface grinding are composed of grits similar to those used on an off-hand grinder but the bonding used is different and special wheels are sold for use on surface grinders. Under no circumstances should a wheel designed for normal off-hand work be used for surface grinding. Bonding is different for various grades of wheels, depending on the grain or grit that is used. Different bonding is also intended for various usages and it is important that the right grade is used for the particular purpose.

It is possible for the model engineer to make small simple surface grinders, the most complicated part being the compound table. It is possible to purchase small tables should that be more convenient than making ones own. It must be possible to adjust the raising and lowering of either the head, or table, within

very fine limits and it must also be possible to lock it rigidly in position. The use of a purchased compound table would create its own problems as they are invariably driven by lead screws, which would have to be discarded in favour of a lever operated movement. The cross travel can remain driven by a lead screw in order to obtain the required fine adjustment.

Although not strictly in the realm of surface grinding, the milling machine can also be used to hold mounted grinding points. These have already been referred to and their use in a milling machine is particularly applicable where shaped section needs to be made, or an extra fine finish is required in a small area of the work. While it may be possible to make such sections with a milling cutter, the cutter is very likely to leave an uneven finish that is undesirable; the mounted point used in this way will leave a mirror finish.

If a milling machine is used for surface grinding then a great deal of care is needed to ensure grinding dust must not enter the mandrel bearings or slides. It is usually practical to prevent dust entering the slides by applying wide masking tape to the table in such a way that that is will act as a skirt over the area where dust could enter. Alternatively if the machine is to be used for grinding on a regular basis it might be worthwhile using strips of leather for the same purpose.

Keeping the work cool

When using a surface grinder best results will be obtained if there is a continuous supply of coolant and this will generally be in the form of soluble oil, which should be pumped onto the work, in order to ensure a sufficient supply. The coolant is used not only to keep the work cool but also to wash away the particles left as the grinding wheel does its work. If there is insufficient suitable coolant, work can become badly marked and scored. It follows therefore that the machine should be fitted with a good coolant supply as well as a means of filtering and re-circulating it. A good supply of coolant is also essential as an aid to accuracy, which may sound rather strange. The very abrasive action of the grinding wheel creates friction and friction creates heat. Follow the chain a little further and heat will cause metal to expand, therefore the work will be expanding during the grinding operation and an allowance will need to be made for it so doing. The supply of coolant if correctly applied will largely prevent the expansion and allow the work to be carried out with greater accuracy. Should the supply be uneven, for example a large quantity at one end of the work and none or virtually none at the other, then the end that has insufficient coolant applied could expand. The grinding wheel will remove more metal from the expanded end than it will from the end that is cool and while we are only talking of tiny amounts, one of the objects of using a surface grinder is to obtain a higher degree of accuracy than is possible with other machines and that extreme accuracy will be lost.

Rotary surface grinding machines

Rotary surface grinding is a different sort of operation altogether - a large diameter wheel that rotates in a horizontal plane is used to generate flat surfaces. The system is used for grinding large flat areas. The wheels are very large, even the smaller ones are at least twelve inches or 300mm diameter and the upper limit anything up to double that diameter. Frequently the grinding material will be a replaceable disk

Surface grinder with a difference, consisting of a sixteen inch diameter wheel. Sometimes the wheel will have special abrasive pads attached to it to do the work. Note on the right, the pipe and control for the coolant supply. It is not unusual for the work to be flooded with coolant during the whole time it is being dealt with.

glued to the wheel. A similar system is often used for production woodworking as well as in metal working shops. Although a work clamp is fitted to the machine it is basically a hand-operated process and the wheel rotates at a much slower speed than is usual with grinding wheels used for metalworking. The wheel is invariably supplied with a pumped supply of coolant and the motor required to drive the wheel is more powerful than that used for normal grinding purposes. The system has the advantage that it is possible to remove large areas of material quite rapidly as the whole of the work is ground at one setting unlike normal surface grinding where even in the case of a vertical machine the area of metal removal is comparatively small. When designed for metalworking purposes these machines invariably include a pumped coolant supply, which is essential for reasons that have already been stated. There is no coolant used when the machines are designed for woodworking purposes and of course a different type of abrasive disk is used.

Frequently this type of machine is fitted with guides or jigs to ensure that the work is held accurately in position and at the correct angle. It is not a process that is very likely to find favour in the home workshop, as machines are bulky and have a very limited use.

Safety

It should go without saying that any form of surface grinding requires the normal safety precautions regarding dress, etc to be observed. There is an additional problem, as even though most machines are fitted with splashguards it seems to be almost inevitable that the operator is going to receive a considerable quantity of cutting fluid on him or herself. It is therefore a good idea to use a waterproof apron when using these machines.

Chapter 8

Cylindrical and Toolpost Grinding

The very name cylindrical grinding is all that is needed to conjure a picture of the type of grinding machine to be dealt with next. A well-executed ground finish on a round bar, or the periphery or inside of a cylinder is about as near to perfection as it is possible to get. No matter how good a lathe might be, or how skilled the operator, the accuracy and finish can never compare with that obtained by grinding. It is the method used throughout the world for hundreds or possibly thousands of different types of component, far too many to even start to name them all. A motorcar will have

A very large cylindrical grinder. Such machines are quite common in industries where this sort of operation takes place.

67

numerous parts that have a ground finish and all the hydraulics of a digging machine will have been ground in order to obtain the required accuracy and finish.

If we take a shaft that has been machined very carefully on a lathe and examine it under a magnifying glass it will be seen that what may very well appear to the naked eye as a perfect finish is in fact little more than a very fine thread. Of course it is too fine to be used as a thread but all

those tiny grooves will cause wear on any mating part. Using the correct grade of grindstone in a cylindrical grinding machine means that there are no grooves and in addition the part can be made to a far higher tolerance.

Cylindrical grinders are specialist machines and certainly are unlikely to be found in many home workshops. They work on the simple principal of rotating the work between centres whilst applying a rotating grindstone to the surface that is being machined. Most work is carried out with fine grinding wheels and a good quantity of coolant liquid is applied. Most modern machines are computer controlled. The wheels used for cylindrical grinding are generally made from aluminium oxide and special grades are available, a popular type being a grade of pink aluminium oxide containing a small quantity of chromium oxide.

Centreless grinding

For an even better ground finish as well

A cylindrical component set up ready for grinding.

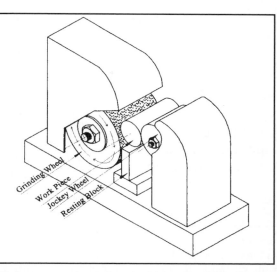

The principle of centre-less grinding. Plenty of coolant is required and a top support to keep the workpiece in place

Grinding Wheel
Work Piece
Jockey Wheel
Resting Block

as greater accuracy, centreless grinding is commonly used. The operation is very similar to cylindrical grinding except that instead of the work being mounted between centres it floats between a roller and the grindstone, while resting on a special, adjustable support. In rare instances the support bar is replaced with another roller. As with cylindrical grinding, it is usual to use wheels of aluminium oxide and large quantities of coolant are applied.

Toolpost grinders

The term toolpost grinding is more or less self-explanatory. It is the name given to the

A large tool post grinder, probably too big for use in the average home workshop.

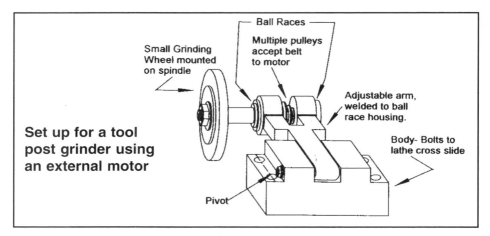

Ball Races

Multiple pulleys
accept belt
to motor

Small Grinding
Wheel mounted
on spindle

Adjustable arm,
welded to ball
race housing.

Body- Bolts to
lathe cross slide

**Set up for a tool
post grinder using
an external motor**

Pivot

use of a small grinding machine located in the toolpost of a lathe and used to carry out various grinding and polishing operations. It could be described as the poor man's cylindrical grinder.

The actual grinding machine can take various forms and usually the size of the lathe will dictate the size and possibly also the versatility of the uses for which the grinder can be used. As far as model engineers are concerned most toolpost grinders will be homemade affairs but professionally made machines are available commercially, although they are generally designed only for use on large lathes.

For many years home made toolpost grinders were rather cumbersome things. Frequently they would be driven by a belt powered from the lathe via some form of lay shaft. Alternatively they would use a large mains motor as a means of obtaining the power. As a rule, both types would have a cluster of three or four pulleys that enabled the rotational speed of the grinder to be changed. These days it is possible to make the grinder much smaller and the use of a lay shaft and belts as a means of drive is virtually obsolete, as it is usual to use low voltage direct current motors, the speed of which can be controlled electronically.

By far the easiest way to make a

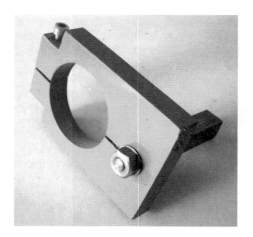

A simple bracket made to accept a mini drill to act as a tool post grinder.

70

The mini drill set up for use as a tool post grinder. A larger drill could be used on a larger machine.

grinder is simply to make a suitable holder for one of the many small power drills that are available. The price and quality of these varies considerably and it is as well to check before buying one to ensure that it is suitable for the purpose for which it is intended. It is also a good idea if buying one to have a look at a number and decide which will be the easiest to adapt for the purpose. This will vary according to the lathe on which it is to be used; the type of grinder that suits one lathe may not be the best type for another make of machine. In most instances the tool will have to fit in some form of cradle and therefore the less complicated the shape of the body the better. There are even some that can be adapted by simply fitting a collar, so looking around will be definitely worthwhile.

Another easy way of making a simple toolpost grinder is to adapt a flexible drive unit. Mainly these are sold for use with the little grinders referred to above but can also be obtained for general use. Their small size generally means that they will fit easily into the toolpost and the adapter required

to secure them therefore is quite easy to make. One of the necessities for a toolpost grinder is that it must be able to rotate, which means the flexible drive will require some form of power unit in order to do this. They can be driven via an ordinary mains powered electric motor of suitable size and this can be anchored somewhere near the base of the lathe. As the drives are usually quite long there is plenty of opportunity to find a suitable location.

The other alternative is to power the drive with the mini drill if that is what it was intended for. Doing so means that a special cradle will have to be made to hold it. This means that it is necessary to make two units to get the grinding spindle in position so that using the flexible drive is not quite as easy as we might have at first believed it to be. Nevertheless the fact that the head of the drive is so small and neat may well mean that it is worth considering the idea.

The voltages at which the machines operate vary. Some are powered direct from the mains supply, while others use a low voltage system. Providing the low voltage system gives sufficient power for one's needs, there is a lot to be said on the grounds of safety for using that type. There is always a danger of damaging or cutting the cable on the mains powered machines and if this happens when it is mounted on the lathe it could result in personal injury or even be fatal. Even if one is lucky enough to avoid actually getting an electric shock, severe damage could be caused to either the lathe or the drill. If a mains unit or motor is to be used it should be connected to the mains via an RCD for safety.

A similar tool post grinder can be made using a normal sized hand held electric drill of the DIY type, but obviously the bulk of the drill makes it more difficult to mount in the toolpost or on the cross slide of most lathes. The biggest problem is getting them at the true centre height, however they have been used with success and certainly are worth consideration if no other option is available. Many, perhaps even the majority of these drills, have a round boss at the front of the body. Frequently this is designed as a means of holding attachments and it can in many cases be used as an anchor point for whatever device is used to mount the drill on the lathe. Here too there is the choice of mains or battery power, the latter being by far the safest option.

The above ideas are a convenient way of making a grinder, but if it is to be used extensively then it is as well to make a tool especially for the job. The time-honoured way is to use a spindle running in ball races and fitted with either a spindle for direct mounting of the wheel, or possibly a chuck. The spindle is the best method as it is then possible to ensure that the stone will be securely held. In the case of the chuck there is always the chance of the mandrel on which the stone is mounted working loose. At the very least this is likely to damage the work piece. The worst scenario is that it could actually be released from the chuck and fly around causing not only damage but also injury.

The spindle can be powered by an electric motor that is mounted on the frame and connected to the spindle via a small belt running in pulleys. As has already been pointed out, a low voltage motor operating on direct current can be electronically controlled obviating the need for multiple pulleys. The pulley system can result in a rather large unit that is unlikely to be suitable for use on one of the very small lathes that are available, but at the same time the unit will be far more rigid and substantial than an electric drill when used with a large lathe.

Some form of guard should be fabricated to cover the wheel and prevent both sparks and dust reaching the operator. It will also provide safety if unfortunately the wheel should break. In addition, some people like to make a transparent cover, which will also protect from dust and as well as allowing the operator to see the work piece. It is also desirable to arrange for some means of getting a good supply of coolant to the work. This can be in some form of gravity system but it is preferable if possible to have a pumped arrangement that will supply the coolant with some amount of force.

Chapter Nine

Honing and Lapping

There are so many similarities in the various processes involved in honing or lapping that it is impossible to separate them. Honing can often be considered as part of the lapping process and lapping part of honing. It is therefore inevitable that there will be some repetition of the processes as described in this chapter. This also applies to the tools involved - a lap can sometimes equally be described as a hone. The important thing is to remember that whatever name the process is called by, it is the art of obtaining the best possible mating finish on an article or in many cases a pair or more of pieces.

Honing falls into several categories. To obtain a good fit for a piston in a cylinder we hone the bore of the cylinder and some people will hone the outside diameter of the piston as well. This process can also be referred to as lapping. It may be that an item will be honed in order to obtain as

perfect a fit as possible between two surfaces that are not circular, typical examples here being the slide valve on a steam cylinder or the slideway on a lathe might be lapped to obtain a good fit to the carriage. There are all sorts of instances when such practices are desirable in order that parts fit together as accurately as possible. As far as honing is concerned, the term is also used to describe methods used to get a really good cutting edge on tools after they have been ground. Honing not only makes the cutting edge keener but also removes any burrs that might have been set up by the grinding actions as well as to give the tool an extra keen edge.

Honing a cutting edge
Tools that are ground in order to sharpen them may appear to the naked eye to be perfect when the grinding process is

A modern honing block of the type used by woodworkers. This example has four different grades of diamond abrasive, one on each side. It is simply lifted from the case and rotated in order to get the required grade for the work on top.

complete, but if they are looked at through a magnifying glass it will be seen that there is invariably a minute burr left by the grinding process. This burr will cause a less than perfect finish to be obtained when the tool is used. By honing it away we not only remove something that is going to leave unwanted marks on machined surfaces but we also add that extra little bit to the sharpness of the tool.

How the honing process is carried out is largely a matter of horses for courses. In other words, different types of tool require different honing techniques. For example the woodworker sharpens his or her chisel or plane iron with a wide slowly revolving grindstone, the whole of the cutting edge being in contact with the stone during the operation. When the tool is subsequently honed it is set at the required angle on a wide stone upon which it is moved too and fro while maintaining the required angle. Some people are happy to carry out this operation by hand; others use a jig or guide that ensures the tool is at exactly the required angle. An improved effect can be obtained when honing without a guide by moving the tool in a figure of eight movement.

This figure of eight movement can be recommended for all work where the tool is taken to the grinding material that is lying flat, while the tool movement is to be by hand. A straightforward up and down

Two grades of diamond hone intended for honing the cutting edges on tools whether for use on wood or metal.

74

A selection of slip stones showing some of the variations available. Different sizes and different shapes suit various jobs. The stones are also available in triangular form. Most are various grades of carborundum; for finer work a stone known an India stone may be used.

movement will almost invariably result in a rocking movement being used, no matter how careful the operator is. The figure of eight movement tends to stop this from happening thus giving a superior finish.

The type of stone that is used for honing will depend largely on individual preference. Various grits can be obtained with all abrasives; some will prefer to use coarser grit than others. It is not unknown for a craftsman to hone the tool twice, using a finer grade of stone on the second occasion. Mention has been made of the need to wash away the worn grits in order the sharper ones are kept at the surface and this applies equally when honing. The majority of stones require the application of a little light oil for this purpose, some sandstones are better used with the addition of water and the same applies to diamond coated stones. The latter should never be used with oil, which has the effect of causing the stone to clog.

Diamond laps are the modern equivalent of the oilstone and like their forebears are available in a variety of grits, if grit is the right word for a collection of small diamonds. As with the various oilstones; the diamond stones are available in a variety of sizes and shapes and their use is well worth consideration.

Generally speaking the finer the edge that a tool has the better it will cut, the only exception being brass; for some reason a very sharp tool can snag when used on it. To give some idea of how almost any material can be used to hone a tool, it is within living memory that men shaved with razors known as cut throats. The name was applied for the very good reason that they were kept so sharp that the slightest slip and blood would be drawn. The edge would be honed with nothing more than a leather strap, which did the job beautifully. The leather strap (always known as a strop) was anchored at one end and the razor was rubbed back and forth on it, the action giving the fine sharp edge that was required.

Honing engineering tools

When talking about honing engineering tools we are mainly concerned with those used on the lathe. Although honing of milling cutters is not unknown, mostly the cutters are used as ground (the rare exception being if a particularly fine finish is required). Lathe tools are likely to be made of three different types of material: high carbon steel; high-speed steel; or one of the hard modern materials such as tungsten carbide, ceramic material or even diamond, although the use of the latter is quite rare.

High carbon steel tools were once the most common but now are quite rare and are usually only found when special cutters are made in the home workshop. In that case it is common to use either silver steel or ground flat stock (gauge plate) and to harden and temper it to suit the work it is to do. As a general rule tools will be made of high-speed steel, which can be bought as either square or round section and ground to the required shape for use on the machine.

Both high carbon and high-speed steel are honed in the same way and the most common material used for doing so is a small oil stone known as a slip stone. These are available in a range of shapes, sizes and grits and initially should be rubbed across the flat areas of the tool with the stone lying flat and parallel to the surface, plenty of oil being applied. As there are at least three surfaces that form the shape on the cutting area of the tool; each has to be done individually. Doing this results in the minutest burr being raised on the cutting edge and a very fine stone should be used at an angle to just remove it. This may seem like blunting the nicely sharpened tool but is in fact just sufficient to give it a keen edge. It is always a good idea to look at the cutting edge through a magnifying glass before using it, to

ensure that it really is good.

It is often a good idea to give the tool a quick going over with a stone during machining operations. Do not remove it from the tool post; leave it in situ and just touch up the cutting edges.

The woodworker generally will be using much larger stones than those used for metal work, because as a rule larger tools are in use. This means it is not practical to take the hone to the tool and so the practice is to set it firmly on a bench. Often it will be securely fitted to a wooden tray as well. The tool is then worked on the stone. In the case of things such as plane irons the tool is frequently of just about the same width as the stone. The fact that the stones are laid on a bench means that it is easy to use a jig or guide set to the correct angle. This ensures that not only is the tool honed at the correct angle but also that pressure is even across the stone

Scribers should never be sharpened with a grindstone; only a hone should be used and the tool should be worked backwards and forwards along the stone. while being slowly rotated at the same time. Sharpening them on a grindstone will almost invariable mean that the temper will be destroyed.

Honing a bore

There is no doubt that a cylinder bore that has been honed will give a vastly improved performance to one that has not. No matter how careful the machine operator is or how good is the tool used to get the final finish on the bore, the end result will be a series of tiny ridges. Even in the case of one that has been reamed the same will apply. Honing will remove these marks, but it will still depend on the quality of the hone as to how good the bore really is. It may well be that some form of progressive honing will be required, using gradually finer grits each time until the required result is achieved.

Various types of hones can be purchased, the majority take the form of three flat stones mounted on arms connected to a central rod. The arms are sprung and the holders of the hones pivot easily. This arrangement ensures that when the hone is put into the bore the stones will lie flat along its face. When using a hone of this type it is essential that it is rotated slowly in the bore and for small work an old-fashioned wheel brace is in many ways the perfect tool as it is easily controlled. For those with a distinct dislike of anything remotely related to hard work it is possible to use a hand held electric drill, but it must be one with a variable speed and the lowest possible speed should be used. One of the battery powered hand drills that are readily available is ideal if power has to be used. As a rule these have a slower speed available than the mains powered type.

The stone must be kept lubricated at all times when the tool is in use. This is essential to avoid scratches on the bore; it also goes some way to preventing both tool and work from overheating. For most purposes light machine oil will suffice as a lubricant but for working on brass or bronze water will often do just as well. When honing aluminium, water is recommended, as oil will tend to clog up the stone. Paraffin should not be used under any circumstances; using it can result in scratches on the work. For an extra fine finish on brass or bronze it was not uncommon for old time craftsmen to lubricate hones with milk which not only cooled things down but also gave a very fine polish.

When using this type of hone it is essential that it is contained in the bore; if it protrudes from the ends, the stones will be liable to tip at an angle due to the springs and the result is an effect known as bell mouthing. The name speaks for itself - the ends become enlarged because of the angular movement of the stones. The hone should be moved backwards and forwards in the bore while it is rotated, taking care of course that it does not come out of the end.

Honing bores can be just as easily carried out with a drilling machine as it can with a hand drill. The action does create a great deal of heat and so it will usually be necessary in either case to hold the work in a vice or clamp it in some way. With the work held in this way if can be infinitely more difficult to line it up accurately with the hone in a drilling machine than to do so by hand. If it is possible to mount the work accurately in the lathe for the operation, the hone can be supported in the tailstock chuck and the lathe rotated in back gear giving the best of both worlds. If doing this it is essential to remove all traces of abrasive afterwards to avoid damage to the bearings and slides of the lathe.

Home-made hones

It may well be that a hone of a suitable size is not readily available and in that case it is not difficult to make one's own and there are a variety of methods of doing so. One important thing to remember when making a hone (whether for a round surface such as a cylinder or a flat one) is that the material used must be softer than the material that is to be honed. The easiest method is to machine a short length of hardwood to the exact size that the bore is to be and then put the slightest of tapers on the end to provide an easy means of entry. Soak the business end of the wood in some light oil and then coat it with a mild abrasive. The abrasive used will largely depend on how much of a polish is needed; in some cases a fine grinding paste of the type used to grind in the valves on the engine of a motorcar is all right. In other cases household scouring powder mixed with a little oil can be used and for a very fine finish, metal polish. This type of hone is used in exactly the same way as those with three stones but providing sufficient length has been machined to the required diameter no harm will come if it is allowed to protrude from the end.

A more sophisticated version is to machine the wood to size in the same way, and then drill a hole centrally along it. It only needs be a very small hole as it is to be used as a pilot for a wood screw. The wood is then slit lengthways using a very fine saw, the narrower the slot is the better. A wood screw is inserted in the central hole and the hone is then used in exactly the same way as shown in the paragraph above. After the first pass through the bore the screw can be tightened a little and this will expand the wood. The only snag with this type of hone is that when the screw is tightened the wooden hone is no longer parallel. It is therefore necessary to move the raised section to each end of the bore as honing takes place.

A third method is to use a similar piece of wood, but this time machined slightly undersized for the bore and make a fine saw cut across the diameter. Insert a short length of abrasive paper in the slot and rotate that in the bore in the same way. Make sure there is sufficient lubricant when doing this and again take the rotating abrasive material right to the ends of the bore while it is in use. If required, two or three grades of material can be used to get a particularly fine result. The idea works quite well. It is necessary to ensure that the material is held tightly in the slot otherwise the pressure of the work will cause it to be dragged out.

Much more sophisticated and as a result requiring more effort to make are copper hones. They do have the advantage that they can be used over and over again. The arbour on which they run is made in three pieces. The outer two are tapered about one and a half degrees and the two sections are drawn together with a threaded rod. The actual lap consists of a length of copper tubing with a series of holes in it. Make sure the burrs are completely removed when making this part. Make a slit through the whole length with a very fine toothed saw and set it between the to tapers. As the thread is tightened the copper will expand to fit the bore. Use plenty of lubricant and a fine abrasive of some sort and the result is as good as any professionally made lap could be.

If a suitable diameter of copper tube is not available a short length of sheet can be rolled to size. Whether tube or sheet is used it helps to thoroughly anneal the copper before use as it will then pick up the shape of the bore.

Lapping
Lapping is the term generally given to the

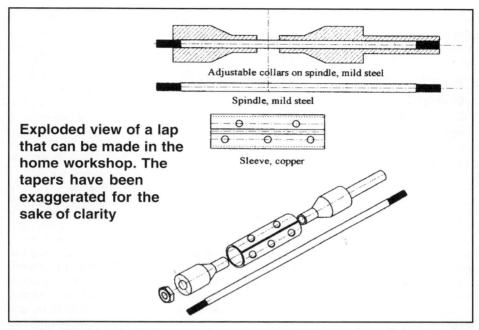

Adjustable collars on spindle, mild steel

Spindle, mild steel

Sleeve, copper

Exploded view of a lap that can be made in the home workshop. The tapers have been exaggerated for the sake of clarity

work involved in obtaining two close mating parts. They may be flat but the term can also be applied to fitting a piston in a bore or some similar exercise. Sometimes the parts to be mated are themselves used to do the work; in other instances each piece is dealt with separately. In theory the latter idea will give the best results but it must depend on each individual job as to the method adopted. For example if we want to lap a piston into a bore, having got both to a good tight fit, the piston can be coated with a mild abrasive paste and gently worked into the cylinder bore. The lapping in this case should be done by gently pushing the piston in for a short distance, ensuring too much pressure is not used. It is then withdrawn, rotated about an eighth of a turn and the operation

repeated. This goes on until the piston has been fully rotated when it is inserted a little deeper and the process of rotation repeated. This is continued with the piston being pushed in deeper each time until the two parts have been lapped over the whole length.

It is not possible to lap a piston in this way into a cylinder that has a closed end. Because of the fit that is being aimed at, air pressure will prevent the piston being pushed right to the top of the bore. We can use this fact to get some idea of the effectiveness of the lapping process when lapping a piston in the bore of a cylinder that is open-ended. When the work is finished, push the piston right home, seal off the end of the cylinder and then try to pull the piston out. If it is a perfect fit and

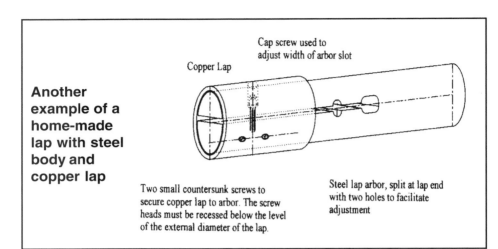

Another example of a home-made lap with steel body and copper lap

Cap screw used to adjust width of arbor slot

Copper Lap

Two small countersunk screws to secure copper lap to arbor. The screw heads must be recessed below the level of the external diameter of the lap.

Steel lap arbor, split at lap end with two holes to facilitate adjustment

the end of the cylinder has really been sealed until airtight, it should be impossible to withdraw the piston. Such a hundred percent fit is unlikely and the amount of effort required to withdraw the piston is an indication of how good the fit is. When it does come out there should be a loud popping noise and the louder this is, the better the fit that has been obtained.

It is essential that before testing and particularly before use, the surfaces of both bore and piston are thoroughly cleaned and all traces of abrasive are removed.

Lapping two flat surfaces together employs exactly the same principle; one surface is coated in a mild grinding paste and the two parts are massaged against each other. Keeping the two parts flat to each other is the difficult part, but it is essential that this is the case. Testing for the fit is done in the same way as with a bore; both surfaces are thoroughly cleaned and then pushed together. In the unlikely circumstances of a perfect fit it will be impossible to separate them. Once again

such a fit is highly improbable but the harder it is to pull the pieces apart the more efficient the lapping process has been. Allowing for the fact that such a fit is most unlikely put a few drops of light oil on one of the finished surfaces and then rub the two parts together before finally aligning them correctly. Assuming a good finish they should be held so firmly together that they cannot be pulled directly apart.

These then are several rules to be followed when lapping and honing. They particularly apply where mating surfaces are required or an extra high quality finish is needed, less so when honing the edge of a tool in order to make it keener.

Diamond laps

Diamond laps have already been referred to; they are the modern version of the slip stone but a few comments on them will do no harm. They are available in a variety of grades and as well as usually being considerably larger they are not available in as many shapes as slip stones. This means that for certain tasks they are not suitable. In the event that one of a suitable size and shape can be found, they are very effective and are particularly effective on tools made of or tipped with carbide.

Although not strictly classed as laps the small abrasive discs sold for use with the little hand drills can be effectively used for the purpose. There are several types available; some are tiny grindstone, but these are best used for purposes other than lapping. The types that are effective for that purpose are either small abrasive disks that are used with a backing pad or very thin diamond coated disks that are ideal for touching up carbide tools.

Chapter 10

Polishing

In the same way that the subjects of honing and lapping overlap each other, so do those two subjects overlap that of polishing. Procedures are very similar; therefore a great deal of polishing work is identical to work involved in honing and lapping.

First let us ask ourselves why we need to polish an object. The obvious answer in general is to improve the appearance and this is true, but we have also polished work when lapping parts together. In fact all we are looking for when it comes to polishing is an improved appearance.

Polishing mops

When youngsters used to be taught metalwork at school, they invariably loved to use the polishing mop. These are calico or cotton disks sewn together to form a circular mop with a central hole, strengthened with a leather disk at either side. Mops are fitted on to a mandrel on a machine; frequently this machine takes the form of an electric motor with a spindle protruding from each end. There are some instances of machines connected to the spindle via pulleys and a belt in order to

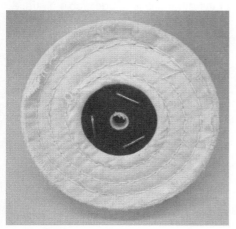

A typical polishing mop. Note the stitches round the mop at regular intervals. This mop is a hard type; softer ones have less rows of stitches and very soft ones no stitching at all.

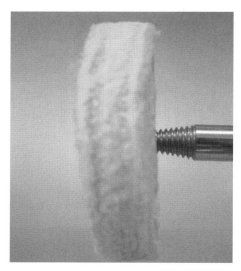

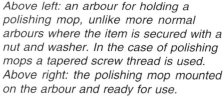

Above left: an arbour for holding a polishing mop, unlike more normal arbours where the item is secured with a nut and washer. In the case of polishing mops a tapered screw thread is used. Above right: the polishing mop mounted on the arbour and ready for use.

give an increase in speed. Unlike the method of fitting a grindstone, the mops are not secured with nuts and washers but are run on to a tapered thread. The thread might be left-handed, depending on which side of the motor it protrudes from, this ensures the effect of running the machine is to tighten the mop rather than remove it. Mops come in a wide variety of types, and the type of stitching is the key as to how hard the finished product will be. Soft ones consist simply of leaves of material joined with a leather or plastic washer in the centre; harder types will have a number of rows of circular stitches at regular intervals.

A polishing compound is held against the mop while it is rotating, the compound during the process becomes impregnated in the mop. There are different compounds designed to work with different metals or to give different finishes and while it is possible to overlay one compound on top of the other this is not desirable as traces of the original will remain and could have a detrimental effect on the work. Generally the compounds or finishing bars, as they are known are available in the following types. *General purpose*, designed mainly for removal of scratches. *Bright shine*, reasonable for scratch removal and also reasonable for polishing. *Mirror finish*, not a great deal of scratch removal properties but will impart a reasonably good polish. *Synthetic gloss* polishing bar, designed to impart a polish on non-ferrous metals. *Steelcut*, designed as the name suggests for imparting a finish on steel. *Vonax*, for polishing plastics of all sorts. In addition

A motor with a double ended shaft. One end has the tapered screw for a mop, the other a more normal fixing with nut and washer. The interesting thing about this set up is the fact that a sponge rubber arbour fitted with a band of polishing material has been mounted on that end.

some bars are sold as pre-finishing products; they do not polish but give a matt or semi matt finish to the work. Some manufacturers of the bars simply describe them by their colour so it is necessary to establish from the tool stockist exactly what is being bought and what it is reasonable to expect it to do.

Having been primed, the work is held against the fast revolving mop. Depending on the compound with which it has been primed, this will remove all but the deepest of scratch marks and when the traces of the polishing compound are removed it will be seen that the work has a reasonably smooth finish. In the meantime the friction involved will have caused the work to become extremely hot and if the operator is not wearing stout leather gloves it will be impossible to handle it. It is a quick and easy way to impart a polish that will generally suit most purposes, but it cannot be described as high quality. No doubt it is

the speed with which the job can be accomplished that accounts for its popularity amongst the schoolchildren, who quickly learned that they can put a nice shine on coins, keys and all sorts of other objects.

The polishing mop therefore does provide a quick way to do things but it has a big disadvantage as it is not possible to accurately control the action of the mop. The result is that the object being polished will be far from flat; in places the mop will have dug deeper into it than in others and during operations the outside edges of the work become bevelled. In many instances this bevelled effect is unimportant and the end result will be quite satisfactory; the fact that the object is not absolutely flat may also be of no consequence. Nevertheless for general polishing it is a quite satisfactory process and is also useful for making a start on items that need a better finish than can be obtained with

A polishing mop mounted on a machine. Note how the composition of the mop has changed by the application of a polishing compound.

the mop.

In addition to calico or cotton, the mops can be obtained made from felt. These are not designed to be used with a compound but they can be successfully used with a cleaner such as a brass or silver polish - a medium used only for imparting a polish. Small mops are also available designed to fit DIY electric drills and they have an arbour permanently fitted. These are generally made from cotton material and like their larger counterparts can be obtained in soft or hard versions. Even smaller felt mops in a number of shapes are available. They are similar to grinding points but are referred to as bobs.

Polishing mediums

It has already been pointed out that polishing with mops will result in bevelled edges and that this can impair the look of an article. Certainly clock makers would shudder at the thought that the polished parts of their clock did not have nice square edges. The answer here is to polish the work on a flat plate using one of the many polishing mediums available on the market sold either in paste form or as powder to be mixed to the consistency one

A Viceroy buffing machine. For reasons of safety the points of the tapered arbours have plugs fitted on them. These plugs are adjustable via the brackets and not only do they protect the operator from damaging him- or herself but they also prevent the polishing mop from coming off during use.

Another example of an industrial machine. Using such machines invariably creates a great deal of mess and dirt and in this case an extra large shield is built in to prevent the surrounding area from dirt and to collect any that is released.

desires. They vary considerably from grit based abrasive pastes to liquids; they are far too numerous to list here and like the compounds described above, the only way is to discuss one's need with a good tool stockist. To add further to the confusion there are also ranges of pastes incorporating diamond powder of various grades that may be an improvement on the grit based type. Any will do the job successfully, providing care and time is taken. The technique has already been described; a quantity of the medium being used is placed on a known flat surface, and the work is laid flat on it and moved in a figure of eight motion on it until the desired effect is achieved. A proper plate designed for the purpose will contain a number of grooves, which will absorb surplus polishing medium. A plain plate will suit most purposes but remember it must be perfectly flat.

By progressively using a finer medium the desired result will be obtained. It is not unusual for four or even five grades of progressively finer medium to be used to obtain the required finish. In the absence of a proper plate it is possible to use a piece of plate glass to do the work. It must be pointed out however that the glass or

A small buffing mop designed for use with a mini drill. The separate sheets are dispensed with and replaced by a series of fibres.

A small self-contained spindle and housing by Picador, designed to be belt driven from a motor and can be obtained with either a double ended pointed screw type spindle or a spindle with the screw at one end and nut and washer fitting at the other.

whatever material is used has to be perfectly flat.

A word of caution here - once grinding paste of any sort has been applied and work started, under no circumstances should further medium be added. If the grinding medium is apparently loosing its power only a suitable liquid should ever be added. The reason for this is that by adding further medium one is introducing new sharp grains to mix with older worn ones and this will result in scratching of the work as the new grains will not be evenly distributed over the polishing plate. The only way is to wipe everything clean and make a fresh start.

This is a good reason for mixing one's own grinding paste as in that case the liquid that is used for making the paste is known and more can be added if required.

A small felt mop. These consist of a shaped section of felt on a spindle and they are available in a number of sizes and shapes. Used with a very fine paste type polishing compound they are quite effective for obtaining a very high finish.

In the case of ready-made pastes that have been purchased it is not possible to be certain of the medium used to make it and therefore adding more liquid can result in the wrong fluid being used. For example if the original mixture was oil based and the new liquid that was added was water, the two would not mix and adding the liquid would just defeat its own purpose.

Some people like to finish the polishing work by using one of the liquid metal polishes on the market. It is highly unlikely that any of these can improve on a job that has been properly done using progressively finer grades of polishing medium. Liquid polishes are generally applied with a cloth and there is a danger that the cloth will pick up pieces of dirt or grit that will be sufficient to cause scratching on the surface of the material being worked on. The best way to get a final finish is to stretch a piece of dry, clean cotton cloth over a perfectly clean flat plate and use the figure of eight motion again to give a final buffing up.

Obtaining a perfect polish is an art in itself and it requires a great deal of time and patience to be really successful.

Chapter Eleven

Barrelling

Although the proper name for this process is barrelling and the machine a barrel, it is far more common for them to be referred to as either a rumbler or tumbler and as the name suggests the device consists of a drum rather like a barrel. It contains a quantity of abrasive material and rough castings are put in it. The drum is rotated under power and the action of the abrasive material removes a certain amount of the rough finish on the casting. This improves its overall appearance; it also can remove the hard outer shell, making machining generally easier. As is always the case,

A small commercially made rumbler or polishing machine. These small machines are generally designed for lapidary work and are unlikely to be robust enough for engineering purposes.

91

the type of abrasive material used must depend on the type of work. The machines are made in all sizes and in industry it is not unusual to see a drum of two metres or more diameter in use, while a maker of jewellery will frequently use a tiny machine with a diameter of no more than three or four centimetres. The main use of the machines for a jeweller is to polish rare stones. The power required to drive the drum is of course in direct relation to the size of it. Many of the machines used in industry, some of which are quite enormous, not only rotate but also have a reciprocating motion designed to give the maximum possible movement to the material being cleaned.

Abrasive materials suitable for use in these machines can be obtained from specialist suppliers and usually contain a medium such as silicon carbide grains in a very coarse form. A common medium is sand and for heavy work a coarse grade with plenty of small sharp stone in it is ideal. Softer types of sand can be used for work that has a less coarse finish. For very fine work scouring powder may be used.

Although sometimes used dry, for best overall results a small quantity of water should be added to the abrasive medium.

On large machines the drum may be belt or gear driven, rotating on a central spindle on smaller ones it is not unusual for the drum to rest on rollers, one of which is indirectly rotated by a motor. It is necessary to have a means of getting both grinding medium and components into the drum and in the case of a large machine this usually means a close-fitting hatch that is secured with bolts and a gasket. Where a smaller drum is concerned a screw-on cover at one end, the other is permanently sealed, an arrangement that is particularly suited to a drum that is rotated by rollers. Most home made machines, which means the majority of those used in amateur workshops, use barrels adapted from normal household items. Typical examples are large jam jars, which are particularly suitable for those interested in making jewellery; for larger operations biscuit barrels or large plastic jars can be used. The important things are that the barrel is round and that the lid is of such a fit that the grinding medium cannot escape during operations. Drums can be made of metal, plastic or even thick glass although obviously glass is best used only when the objects to be rotated are very small.

Bearings should if possible be either ball races or needle rollers; if this is not

The same machine as in the previous picture but the barrel has been replaced by a large glass jar with a screw on lid.

possible and friction bearings are used, they must be very free running. No attempt should be made to obtain a good bearing fit and a bit of slop will do no harm at all. We are not looking for a precision fit but for something as free running as possible.

It is usual to use a belt or toothed belt as a means of driving the rollers, although in some cases a friction drive directly on to one of the rollers is used. It is essential that the final rotation of the rollers is quite slow and it is therefore necessary to introduce some form of reduction in the drive. This has another advantage as the amount of power required to drive the rollers will be reduced.

It is impossible to suggest suitable motors as the range available is so wide; however it is certainly not necessary to use a large powerful mains motor. As only a low power is needed it follows that the motor used can be quite small, ideally one with a built in reduction gear box. Alternatively the type used on sewing machines or those used to power extraction fans will be quite powerful enough to drive even a quite large drum. It

also means that the machine is suitable for driving with a low voltage motor in which case it is possible to introduce speed control. While a change of rotational speed is unlikely to be needed it does mean that a suitable speed can be set electronically. It is not unknown for old motors from cars to be pressed into service; in particular those used to operate electrically controlled windows. The use of twelve volts gives an added safety factor to the operation.

The rollers on most machines will be suitable for use with several different drums; there is little point in putting a very small item in a large drum and having to use a large quantity of grinding medium. Within reason a gap between the rollers of around three to four inches or seventy five to a hundred millimetres will be suitable. If this is not going to suffice for the work envisaged, it is not too difficult to make the gap between rollers adjustable. Providing the drum is not going to tip over the end, the length of the rollers will not be of great importance but it will of course be necessary to ensure that the frame on which they are mounted does not protrude in such a way that it will foul the drum as it rotates.

The material from which the rollers are made is not all that important; they can be of wood, plastic or metal. Pieces of broom handles will suffice for smaller machines, plastic drain piping for larger ones. Anyone wanting to use metal rollers might consider the use of piece of scaffold tubing. The disadvantage of metal rollers is the additional weight involved and this should be considered. If the machine is to stand in a permanent position the extra weight may be an advantage is it will keep it steady when in use; if it is to be portable plastic will be better

There is no hard and fast rule regarding the quantity of grinding medium that is used. Somewhere between a sixth and a quarter full usually does the trick, but it is essential that the medium is wet enough to flow while at the same time not consisting of all liquid and little grinding material. Somewhere around the consistency of yoghurt appears to be about right. Smaller items need the material to be slightly more fluid than larger ones. It can be reused time and time again until completely spent but will need to be changed for one of different texture if a variety of items are to be dealt with.

Machines can be bought from suppliers of equipment for lapidary work most are rather small and would not be suitable for dealing with larger castings. Those designed for work in engineering are much harder to find and it is unlikely that one suitable for use in a home workshop would be available.

Chapter 12

Safety when Grinding

As with all operations the question of safety both for the operator and other people is of the utmost importance. Operations involving the use of abrasives by their very nature involves the release of dust that contains particles of the abrasive material an in addition can also be highly toxic. When a machine of any sort is used for grinding a shower of sparks will be emitted. Those sparks are in fact red-hot pieces of material coming away from both the abrasive and the work. By their very nature they are tiny and therefore soon loose their heat, but this does not mean they cannot burn. In addition the particles are so fine that they amount to a form of dust and if taken into the lungs could easily be a cause of serious illnesses. We are therefore beholden to take every precaution to guard against these problems.

Guards

All grinding machines should incorporate a safety guard, which should be in place, whenever the machine is in use. The guard should be strong enough and of sufficient size to protect the operator and anyone else in the workshop from danger in the event of a grinding wheel shattering. Wheels do shatter and when they do the result is small pieces flying off with great velocity; these are capable of doing considerable damage and causing serious injury.

Protection from dust

While a guard will also protect the operator from some of the sparks that will be coming from the work, it will not be any sort of protection from dust and some form of personal protection against this is essential. For the home workshop a simple facemask will be sufficient; in a commercial workshop a mask with a filter is necessary.

The machine guard will not provide complete protection from the sparks that are thrown out and remember these are in fact small particles of red-hot material. It is therefore necessary to wear protective glasses or better still a complete transparent facemask. For industrial purposes it is usual to combine mask and safety glasses as a single unit. This would also be an ideal form of protection in a home workshop.

When using the off hand grinder the work is almost certain to be held by hand, so the hands become vulnerable to the hot sparks. This means gloves should always be worn and they should never be made of a man-made material as most materials of that type can dissolve in heat. In addition to the problem of sparks the work will become hot from the friction involved. Indeed it can become red hot if allowed to do so, although it is very bad practice to allow that much heat to be generated. Suitable gloves will protect from both sparks and hot metal. The best types are made of leather, but good stout cotton ones will do if leather is not available.

Clothing

It is very tempting on a hot day to wear just a shirt in the workshop in order to keep cool, something which should never be done when grinding as once again we have the problem of hot sparks being generated. They can make their way through thin material, particularly man made fibres and are therefore a source of danger. A good overall coat will usually offer sufficient protection for most jobs, but if a large amount of work with abrasives is to be undertaken a coat is advisable.

Hair is another thing that can be a problem during grinding operations. The wearing of a hat is strongly advised. This will prevent hot particles settling into one's hair and in addition will prevent the hair from trapping a large quantity of dirt and dust from the grinding operation.

Abrasive disks

It is virtually impossible to introduce a safety guard when using abrasive material in a portable drill. All the products referred to for use in that way therefore introduce an extra degree of danger to the operator. Safety precautions must therefore be in the form of personal clothing, plus plenty of good old-fashioned common sense.

Be prepared

All workshops should possess some first aid equipment, in case of emergency. If grinding is to be carried out to any extent this must include a means of dealing with burns. There must also be at least one quick and easy means of escape. If possible more than one and some means of communicating with somebody outside of the workshop so that help can be summoned in the event of a serious accident. It is a good idea to arrange if possible to contact someone outside at regular intervals so that if contact is not made investigations can start to see if anything has gone wrong. After all if one is overcome by fumes or something similar then it will be impossible to summon help. Safety is largely a matter of common sense and many people spend hours on end contenting themselves in home workshops without mishap.

Index